Taste of Home
EVERYDAY
AIR FRYER

100+ RECIPES FOR WEEKNIGHT EASE : VOLUME 2

Visit us at **tasteofhome.com** for other
Taste of Home books and products.

International Standard Book Number:
978-1-62145-807-4

Executive Editor: Mark Hagen
Senior Art Director: Raeann Thompson
Editor: Amy Glander
Designer: Carrie Peterson
Deputy Editor, Copy Desk: Dulcie Shoener
Copy Editor: Kara Dennison
Deputy Editor, Culinary: James Schend

Cover
Photographer: Mark Derse
Set Stylist: Stacey Genaw
Food Stylist: Josh Rink

Pictured on front cover and title page:
Chicken Parmesan, p. 152
Pictured on title page:
Lemon Pepper Broccoli, p. 78
Pictured on back cover:
Barbecue Chicken, p. 167; Mocha Cupcakes, p. 243;
Eggs Lorraine, p. 65; Loaded Hash Browns, p. 58;
Veggie Burgers, p. 112; Sausage Pizzas, p. 140

INSTANT POT® is a trademark of
Double Insight Inc. This publication has
not been authorized, sponsored or
otherwise approved by
Double Insight Inc.

Printed in China
3 5 7 9 10 8 6 4 2

CONTENTS

AIR FRYER 101 ▪ 4

SNACKS & APPETIZERS ▪ 8

BREAKFAST & BRUNCH ▪ 40

SIDE DISHES ▪ 68

FISH, SEAFOOD & MEATLESS ▪ 102

PORK ENTREES ▪ 126

POULTRY ENTREES ▪ 146

BEEF ENTREES ▪ 178

SANDWICHES ▪ 204

SWEETS & DESSERTS ▪ 230

INDEX ▪ 254

COMMON AIR-FRYER MISTAKES ▪ 256

MORE WAYS TO CONNECT WITH US:

SAY GOODBYE TO YOUR DEEP FRYER, AND PREPARE THE CRISPIEST, CRUNCHIEST, TASTIEST "UNFRIED" FOODS EVER. LET THIS BOOK BE YOUR GUIDE.

Do you love kitchen gadgets? If the answer is yes, chances are you have an air fryer. These small but mighty countertop appliances have been around for about a decade, but they've recently picked up steam for their ability to "fry" foods with little to no oil.

AIR-FRYING TIP

Have a favorite oven-cooked meal that you would like to make in the air fryer? Reduce the suggested temperature by 25°F and then cut the cook time by about 20%. Use the pause button to occasionally check for doneness.

If you're new to this method of "frying" food, fear not. Now you can cook with confidence with the 116 delicious air-fried recipes inside *Taste of Home Everyday Air Fryer Volume 2*. With this new cookbook, it's never been easier to lighten some of your favorite comfort foods. That's because the air method practically eliminates the need for oil, leaving you with crispy breaded chicken, crab rangoon, calamari, pizza puffs, sweet potato chips and other fun foods, all without the unpleasant mess or excess fat of deep-fat frying.

But this appliance isn't just for creating a healthier alternative to cooking traditionally deep-fried foods. You can also make other tried-and-true favorites with this cool tool. Cook up a juicy air-fryer steak. Start your Saturday morning with a batch of sizzling sausage bacon bites. Or satisfy your sweet tooth with air-fried cheesecake or cookies.

Air-fryer aficionados know this kitchen tool is good for more than making recipes from scratch. It's also awesome for reheating foods such as burgers, french fries and other takeout faves. Put it to work cooking your favorite frozen foods—from potatoes and veggies to meat—in a flash. The possibilities are endless!

HOW DOES IT WORK?

An air fryer is basically a mini countertop convection oven. The food goes into a basket (similar to the one you'd use in a deep fryer), but instead of hot oil, the food is blasted with hot air to create the crunchy texture that everyone craves.

Because of its small size, air fryers heat up fast. An air fryer is ready to cook after about three minutes of heating.

The main unit holds a heating coil and a fan, and food is placed in the removable fryer basket below. Hot air rushes down and around the food in the basket. This rapid circulation makes the food crisp, as deep-frying does, with little or no added oil.

Some air fryers have digital screens with the setting options; others have simple time and temperature dials. Choose the style you are most comfortable using.

Certain air fryers can perform additional functions besides air-frying. These models are often more expensive and larger in size. Choose the one that best suits your needs.

Many models are sized to cook for one or two people. Some have a larger capacity, allowing you to cook for up to four people at a time.

With a smaller appliance, you have to cook in batches, so be sure to account for that in your planning.

Read the instruction manual before getting started.

Remove all packing materials and tape from both outside and inside the appliance. Look up into the heating element (see photos on page 6) to make sure no stray material is lodged in the coil or fan. This can cause the appliance to smoke.

Thoroughly wipe down the heating coil before the first use to remove any residue.

(see photos on page 6)

COOK LIKE A PRO

- Verify the temperature, as it will vary among models, just as it does with ovens. Test your air fryer before using to see if it runs above or below the selected temperature setting.

- Allow plenty of room. Cook food in a single layer, with room for air to circulate. For crispy results, do not forget to flip, rotate or shake the basket's contents halfway through the cooking time.

- Use a thermometer when cooking meat. Air-fried meats brown nicely, so it may look done before reaching an appropriate temperature on the inside.

AIR-FRYER PARTS

A. Heating coil (also shown bottom right)

B. Fan (inside unit)

C. Basket

D. Maximum fill line

E. Temperature setting

F. Time setting

G. Power

H. Basket release

HOW TO CLEAN YOUR AIR FRYER

Basket: The basket, its holder and any dividing compartments that came with your air fryer are dishwasher safe. After each use, allow the air fryer to cool. Remove the cooled basket, tray and pan, and wash them as you would any other dish.

Exterior: When it comes to cleaning the outside of an air fryer, a simple soapy wipe-down will do. Unplug the appliance and gently wipe with a damp cloth. That's it!

Heating Coil: If any oil or residue is on the heating coil, let the unplugged machine cool, then wipe the coil with a damp cloth—just as you would with the heating element on an electric stove.

Unexpected Mess? If your cooking project was a bit messier than usual or the machine has developed an odd odor, your air fryer may require a deeper cleaning.

HERE'S WHAT THE BUTTONS ON YOUR AIR FRYER ACTUALLY MEAN

Thanks to the weeknight-changing magic of air fryers, you can serve up a meal in minutes. Plus, you can cook almost everything in this gadget—from cheesy mozzarella sticks to a plate of Chicken Parmesan. It's basically a home cook's dream come true.

The best reason to jump on the air-fryer bandwagon is the intuitiveness of the most popular models. To help you become an air-fryer pro, we're breaking down the buttons and functions you'll find on most of the handy ovens. Use this helpful guide to master the air fryer's most common functions.

▶|| Button

The Cook/Pause button is one you'll find on compact models like this. This important button allows you to pause cooking so you can turn food (say, chicken wings or fish fillets) to ensure everything is cooked all the way through. It also lets you shake the contents of the basket (fries, broccoli, Tater Tots, etc.) to achieve maximum crispiness. Use this button to check the temperature for doneness when cooking meat, poultry or fish.

-/+ Button

Look for single or dual -/+ buttons to adjust time and temperature. On many popular models, there is a button to shift from time or temperature to adjust both. On models without an LCD screen, the -/+ buttons are replaced by knobs or dials.

Keep Warm

Many home cooks use the air fryer like a second oven, cooking up a tasty appetizer or side dish to go along with the entree baking away in the actual oven. This Keep Warm function does exactly that for a set amount of time—usually 30 minutes.

Food Presets

You may own an air fryer with buttons for certain foods, including frozen french fries, chicken or fish. If you're an air-fryer newbie, they can certainly give you an idea of what to cook in your new machine! The presets give you the ability to cook whatever you want without second-guessing because the temperature and time are already set.

Before setting and forgetting, it's helpful to check out your machine's manual. Every preset is set for a specific amount of food in grams, so for a double serving of chicken—or a smaller amount of frozen fries—you will need to adjust for time.

Roast or Broil

The option to roast vegetables or brown meat in an air fryer is becoming more common with larger air fryer models. Use the Roast setting when you're ready to place a marinated piece of meat—let's say a beef chuck roast—into the air-fryer basket. In a conventional oven, you would typically brown the meat before baking. With an air fryer, you can skip that step. The constant flow of hot air creates a gorgeous, caramelized exterior on its own. Just remember to flip the meat and/or vegetables halfway through. Check the interior temps to know when it's ready to take out, too.

Dehydrate

Dehydrating typically can be done in an air fryer, with food placed on an air-fryer rack. With the Dehydrate option, you can create your own dried fruit or beef jerky right at home! This preset option cooks and dries food using a lower temperature for hours.

CHAPTER 1

SNACKS & APPETIZERS

Crunch into those air-fried appetizers without the guilt of snacking on deep-fried food! Serve up juicy chicken wings, stringy mozzarella cheese sticks and other tasty bites guaranteed to satisfy your cravings.

SCOTCH EGGS

These Scotch eggs are amazing right out of the air fryer when they're hot, but I also love eating them cold for a snack before a soccer or baseball game.
—*Dorothy Smith, El Dorado, AR*

PREP: 10 MIN. • COOK: 15 MIN. • MAKES: 6 SERVINGS

1 lb. bulk pork sausage
  Salt and pepper to taste
6 hard-boiled large eggs
1 large egg, lightly beaten
¾ cup crushed cornflakes

1. Preheat air fryer to 400°. Divide sausage into 6 portions; flatten and sprinkle with salt and pepper. Shape each portion around a peeled hard-boiled egg. Roll in beaten egg, then in cornflake crumbs.

2. Place in a single layer on greased tray in air-fryer basket. Cook until meat is no longer pink, turning halfway through, 12-15 minutes.

1 egg: 313 cal., 22g fat (7g sat. fat), 258mg chol., 614mg sod., 11g carb. (2g sugars, 0 fiber), 17g pro.

TEST KITCHEN TIP: It's traditional to serve Scotch eggs with a dipping sauce—in Britain, it's most often a spicy mustard-based sauce. But you can pair them with your own preferred sauce as well.

CRAB AU GRATIN SPREAD

I serve this warm, comforting appetizer any time we have a get-together
with family or friends. It's easy to whip up with convenient canned crab.
—*Suzanne Zick, Maiden, NC*

PREP: 20 MIN. • COOK: 10 MIN. • MAKES: ABOUT 2 CUPS

2 Tbsp. plus 1 tsp.
  butter, divided
3 Tbsp. all-purpose flour
½ tsp. salt
⅛ tsp. paprika
½ cup half-and-half cream
½ cup whole milk
¼ cup white wine or
  chicken broth
1 can (6 oz.) crabmeat,
  drained, flaked and
  cartilage removed or ⅔ cup
  chopped imitation crabmeat
1 can (4 oz.) mushroom
  stems and pieces,
  drained and chopped
1½ tsp. minced chives
½ cup shredded
  cheddar cheese
1 Tbsp. dry bread crumbs
  Assorted crackers and
  fresh vegetables

1. In a large saucepan, melt 2 Tbsp. butter. Stir in flour, salt and paprika until smooth. Gradually add cream, milk and wine. Bring to a boil; cook and stir until thickened, 1-2 minutes. Stir in crab, mushrooms and chives; heat through. Stir in cheese just until melted. Transfer to a greased shallow 1-qt. baking dish that fits in air fryer.

2. Preheat air fryer to 375°. Melt remaining 1 tsp. butter; toss with bread crumbs. Sprinkle over crab mixture. Place dish in air fryer. Cook until bubbly, 8-10 minutes. Let stand for 5 minutes. Serve with crackers and vegetables. If desired, sprinkle with additional minced chives.

2 Tbsp.: 64 cal., 4g fat (2g sat. fat), 23mg chol., 201mg sod., 2g carb. (1g sugars, 0 fiber), 4g pro.

SWEET POTATO CHIPS

Making homemade sweet potato chips in your air fryer is so quick and easy. Be sure to give the sweet potato slices a quick soak in cold water to help remove some of the excess starch.
—*Elizabeth Godecke, Chicago, IL*

PREP: 20 MIN. • BAKE: 15 MIN./BATCH • MAKES: 12 SERVINGS (1½ CUPS DIP)

2   to 3 large sweet potatoes (1¾ lbs.), peeled and cut into ⅛-in. slices
2   Tbsp. canola oil
1   tsp. chili powder
½   tsp. garlic powder
½   tsp. taco seasoning
¼   tsp. salt
¼   tsp. ground cumin
¼   tsp. pepper
⅛   tsp. cayenne pepper

DIP
¾   cup mayonnaise
½   cup sour cream
2   oz. cream cheese, softened
4½   tsp. minced fresh cilantro
1½   tsp. lemon juice
½   tsp. celery salt
⅛   tsp. pepper

1. Place sweet potatoes in a large bowl; cover with cold water. Let stand 20 minutes. Drain; pat dry.

2. Preheat air fryer to 360°. In a small bowl, mix the oil and seasonings; drizzle over potatoes and toss to coat.

3. In batches, arrange sweet potatoes in a single layer on greased tray in air-fryer basket. Cook until golden brown, 15-20 minutes.

4. In a small bowl, beat dip ingredients until blended. Serve with chips.

½ cup chips with about 2 Tbsp. dip: 285 cal., 16g fat (4g sat. fat), 8mg chol., 217mg sod., 33g carb. (14g sugars, 4g fiber), 3g pro.

AIR-FRYING TIP

The best way to ensure your sweet potato chips come out crispy is to cook them in a single layer in the air fryer. That way, there will be plenty of air circulation to help each chip cook evenly and achieve the crunch you desire.

CRISPY CHICKEN WINGS

You can't go wrong with air-fried chicken wings on game day or any time a craving calls. Our homemade spice rub has a nice kick from the cayenne seasoning.
—Taste of Home *Test Kitchen*

PREP: 15 MIN. • COOK: 35 MIN./BATCH • MAKES: 2 DOZEN

2 tsp. garlic powder
1 tsp. garlic salt
1 tsp. each ground mustard, ginger and nutmeg
½ tsp. pepper
½ tsp. ground allspice
½ tsp. baking soda
½ tsp. cayenne pepper
12 whole chicken wings (2½ lbs.)
Optional: Ranch salad dressing, Buffalo sauce or barbecue sauce

1. Preheat air fryer to 300°. In a large bowl, combine the garlic powder, garlic salt, mustard, ginger, nutmeg, pepper, allspice, baking soda and cayenne.

2. Cut chicken wings into 3 sections; discard wing tip sections. Add to bowl with spices and stir to coat. In batches, arrange wings in a single layer on greased tray in air-fryer basket. Cook 15 minutes. Increase temperature to 400°; cook until chicken juices run clear and wings are golden brown, 20-25 minutes. Repeat with remaining wings. Serve hot with salad dressing or sauce if desired.

1 piece: 54 cal., 4g fat (1g sat. fat), 15mg chol., 102mg sod., 0 carb. (0 sugars, 0 fiber), 5g pro.

HAM & BRIE PASTRIES

Fancy appetizers don't have to be difficult. In fact, this recipe proves it's easy to make something impressive. You can prep these pastries ahead of time and pop them into the air fryer just as your guests arrive.

—Jenn Tidwell, Fair Oaks, CA

PREP: 15 MIN. • COOK: 15 MIN./BATCH • MAKES: 16 PASTRIES

1 sheet frozen
  puff pastry, thawed
⅓ cup apricot preserves
4 slices deli ham, quartered
8 oz. Brie cheese,
  cut into 16 pieces

1. Preheat air fryer to 350°. On a lightly floured surface, unfold puff pastry. Roll pastry to a 12-in. square; cut into sixteen 3-in. squares. Place 1 tsp. preserves in center of each square; top with ham, folding it as necessary, and cheese. Overlap 2 opposite corners of pastry over filling; pinch tightly to seal.

2. In batches, place in a single layer on greased tray in air-fryer basket. Cook until golden brown, 14-15 minutes. Cool 5 minutes before serving. If desired, serve with additional apricot preserves.

Freeze option: Freeze cooled pastries in a freezer container, separating layers with waxed paper. To use, reheat pastries in a preheated 350° air fryer until heated through.

1 appetizer: 144 cal., 8g fat (3g sat. fat), 17mg chol., 192mg sod., 13g carb. (3g sugars, 1g fiber), 5g pro.

AIR-FRYING TIP
Regular mozzarella cheese, cut into 4x½-in. sticks, can be substituted for the string cheese.

MOZZARELLA STICKS

Deep-fried mozzarella sticks are one of our favorite appetizers. I figured out how to make them at home without having to haul out my deep fryer. Make sure to double-bread each one so they get nice and crunchy, and to keep the cheese from oozing out as they get warm.

—Mary Merchant, Barre, VT

PREP: 15 MIN. + FREEZING • COOK: 10 MIN. • MAKES: 1 DOZEN

3 Tbsp. all-purpose flour
2 large eggs
1 Tbsp. water
1 cup dry bread crumbs
2½ tsp. Italian seasoning
½ tsp. garlic powder
⅛ tsp. pepper
12 sticks string cheese
   Cooking spray
1 cup marinara sauce
   or meatless pasta
   sauce, warmed

1. Place flour in a shallow bowl. In another shallow bowl, beat eggs and water. In a third shallow bowl, combine bread crumbs, Italian seasoning, garlic powder and pepper. Coat cheese sticks with flour, then dip in egg mixture and coat with bread crumb mixture. Repeat egg and bread crumb coatings. Cover and freeze for at least 2 hours or overnight.

2. Preheat air fryer to 400°. Place cheese in a single layer on greased tray in air-fryer basket; spritz with cooking spray. Cook until golden brown and heated through, 6-8 minutes, turning halfway through cooking and spritzing with additional cooking spray. Allow to stand 3-5 minutes before serving. Serve with marinara or pasta sauce for dipping.

1 appetizer: 148 cal., 8g fat (4g sat. fat), 46mg chol., 384mg sod., 10g carb. (2g sugars, 1g fiber), 11g pro.

BACON-WRAPPED ASPARAGUS

I serve these bacon-wrapped spears with grilled meat and
sliced fresh tomatoes for a wonderful meal.
—*Trisha Kitts, Dickinson, TX*

TAKES: 30 MIN. • MAKES: 10 SERVINGS

10 fresh asparagus
spears, trimmed
Cooking spray
⅛ tsp. pepper
5 bacon strips,
halved lengthwise

1. Preheat air fryer to 400°. Coat asparagus with cooking spray. Sprinkle with pepper; turn to coat. Wrap a bacon piece around each spear; secure ends with toothpicks.

2. Place asparagus on greased tray in air-fryer basket. Cook until bacon is crisp, 8-10 minutes on each side. Discard toothpicks.

1 appetizer: 25 cal., 2g fat (1g sat. fat), 4mg chol., 74mg sod., 1g carb. (0 sugars, 0 fiber), 2g pro.

WHY YOU'LL LOVE IT...
*"We make this often as an appetizer for get-togethers.
I drizzle a tiny bit of sesame oil on the asparagus and use
freshly ground pepper. Wrap the bacon around 3-4 times.
Thinly sliced bacon works best with this recipe."*
—COOKIEMOUSE, TASTEOFHOME.COM

VEGETARIAN STUFFED MUSHROOMS

These are always a hit at parties and no one misses the meat. Vegetarian soy crumbles, mixed with a blend of parsley, basil, oregano and bread crumbs, make a delightful addition to these savory stuffed mushrooms.
—*Arline Aaron, Brooklyn, NY*

PREP: 15 MIN. • COOK: 10 MIN./BATCH • MAKES: 14 APPETIZERS

14 large fresh mushrooms
1 small onion, finely chopped
4 tsp. canola oil
¾ cup soft bread crumbs
½ cup frozen vegetarian meat crumbles, thawed
1 tsp. minced fresh parsley
1 tsp. dried basil
½ tsp. dried oregano
½ tsp. salt
½ tsp. pepper
   Cooking spray
   Chopped fresh basil, optional

1. Remove stems from mushrooms and chop; set mushroom caps aside. In a large nonstick skillet over medium-high heat, cook and stir stems and onion in oil until tender. Stir in bread crumbs, meat crumbles and seasonings; cook until the bread crumbs are lightly browned. Remove from heat; cool slightly.

2. Preheat air fryer to 350°. Spoon stuffing into mushroom caps. In batches, place in a single layer on greased tray in air-fryer basket; spritz with cooking spray. Cook until heated through and mushrooms are tender, 8-10 minutes. If desired, top with chopped fresh basil. Serve warm.

1 stuffed mushroom: 31 cal., 2g fat (0 sat. fat), 0 chol., 112mg sod., 3g carb. (0 sugars, 0 fiber), 1g pro. **Diabetic exchanges:** ½ starch, ½ fat.

CRAB RANGOON

I always order crab Rangoon at restaurants that serve it—the appetizer is one of my favorites. I decided to create a healthier version at home.
—*Emily Higgins, Wingdale, NY*

PREP: 30 MIN. • COOK: 5 MIN./BATCH • MAKES: ABOUT 3 DOZEN

1 pkg. (8 oz.) reduced-fat cream cheese
½ cup mayonnaise
2 green onions, sliced
1 tsp. paprika
1 Tbsp. lime juice
1 tsp. garlic powder
1 tsp. reduced-sodium soy sauce
8 oz. fresh crabmeat
40 wonton wrappers
Cooking spray
Chinese-style mustard

1. In a small bowl, beat cream cheese and mayonnaise. Stir in green onions, paprika, lime juice, garlic powder and soy sauce. Fold in crab.

2. Preheat air fryer to 350°. Spoon 2 tsp. filling in the center of a wonton wrapper. (Cover remaining wrappers with a damp paper towel until ready to use.) Moisten wrapper edges with water. Fold opposite sides over filling, pressing centers together to seal. Repeat with the remaining sides, making a 4-pointed star. Repeat.

3. In batches, place wontons in a single layer on greased tray in air-fryer basket; spritz with cooking spray. Cook until golden brown and crispy, 5-8 minutes. Serve with mustard.

1 appetizer: 62 cal., 3g fat (1g sat. fat), 11mg chol., 111mg sod., 5g carb. (0 sugars, 0 fiber), 2g pro.

PUMPKIN SHAKARPARA

Shakarparas are crispy fried Indian cookies. My Indian American family makes these traditional treats every year for the holidays. I wanted to put my own twist on them, so I adapted the original recipe by adding pumpkin and fall spices.
—*Jessica Burke, Chandler, AZ*

PREP: 30 MIN. + STANDING • COOK: 5 MIN./BATCH • MAKES: 7½ DOZEN

2 cups all-purpose flour
¾ cup sugar
½ cup semolina flour
1 Tbsp. pumpkin pie spice
1 tsp. ground cloves
¼ tsp. baking powder
½ cup canned pumpkin
1 large egg,
   room temperature
1 Tbsp. butter, melted

1. In a large bowl, whisk the first 6 ingredients. In another bowl, beat the pumpkin, egg and butter until blended. Stir into the dry ingredients to form a soft dough.

2. Turn dough onto a floured surface; knead until smooth, about 12 times. Cover and let rest 15 minutes. Divide the dough into 4 portions. Roll each portion to ⅛-in. thickness. Cut into ½-in. diamonds.

3. Preheat air fryer to 375°. In batches, arrange diamonds in a single layer on greased tray in air-fryer basket. Cook until edges are golden brown, 3-4 minutes. Remove to a wire rack to cool.

1 cookie: 23 cal., 0 fat (0 sat. fat), 2mg chol., 3mg sod., 5g carb. (2g sugars, 0 fiber), 1g pro.

BACON-WRAPPED TATER TOTS

These bacon-wrapped bites are always a hit with my friends and family.
They'll go fast, so you may want to double the recipe!
—*Joni Hilton, Rocklin, CA*

PREP: 30 MIN. • COOK: 15 MIN./BATCH • MAKES: 32 APPETIZERS

16 bacon strips,
    halved lengthwise
½ cup maple syrup
1 tsp. crushed
    red pepper flakes
32 frozen Tater Tots, thawed

1. Preheat air fryer to 400°. In batches, cook bacon on greased tray in air-fryer basket until partially cooked but not crisp, 4-5 minutes. Remove to paper towels to drain; keep warm.

2. Combine syrup and pepper flakes. Dip each bacon piece in syrup mixture, then wrap around a Tater Tot. Secure with toothpicks.

3. Place on greased tray in air-fryer basket. Cook until bacon is crisp, 8-10 minutes.

1 appetizer: 52 cal., 3g fat (1g sat. fat), 4mg chol., 123mg sod., 6g carb. (3g sugars, 0 fiber), 2g pro.

TEST KITCHEN TIP: In order for the meat and fat in your bacon to cook evenly, they have to be at the same temperature. The fat retains the cold longer than the meat, so letting the bacon sit at room temp for 15 minutes before you cook it will help produce a more evenly cooked piece of bacon.

PIZZA PUFFS

I love pizza in any form, so it seemed only logical to turn it into an appetizer. These little bundles can be made ahead of time and chilled until you're ready to pop them into the air fryer.

—Vivi Taylor, Middleburg, FL

PREP: 20 MIN. • COOK: 10 MIN./BATCH • MAKES: 20 SERVINGS

1 loaf (1 lb.) frozen pizza dough, thawed
20 slices pepperoni
8 oz. part-skim mozzarella cheese, cut into 20 cubes
¼ cup butter
2 small garlic cloves, minced
Dash salt
Marinara sauce, warmed
Optional: Crushed red pepper flakes and grated Parmesan cheese

1. Preheat air fryer to 350°. Shape dough into 1½-in. balls; flatten into ⅛-in.-thick circles. Place 1 pepperoni slice and 1 cheese cube in center of each circle; wrap dough around pepperoni and cheese. Pinch edges to seal; shape into a ball. Repeat with the remaining dough, cheese and pepperoni.

2. In batches, place seam side up in a single layer on greased tray in air-fryer basket; cook until light golden brown, 6-8 minutes. Cool slightly.

3. Meanwhile, in a small saucepan, melt butter over low heat. Add garlic and salt, taking care not to brown butter or garlic; brush over puffs. Serve with marinara sauce; if desired, sprinkle with red pepper flakes and Parmesan.

Freeze option: Cover and freeze unbaked pizza puffs on waxed paper-lined baking sheets until firm. Transfer puffs to a freezer container; seal and return to freezer. To use, preheat air fryer to 350°; bake pizza puffs on greased tray in air-fryer basket as directed, increasing time as necessary until golden brown.

1 pizza puff: 120 cal., 6g fat (3g sat. fat), 15mg chol., 189mg sod., 11g carb. (1g sugars, 0 fiber), 5g pro.

KALE CHIPS

Harvesttime means big bunches of kale from local farmers. These crunchy kale chips are delicious, super healthy and easy to make. I season them to take the flavor up a notch. For extra zip, add a dash of cayenne pepper.
—*Luanne Asta, Hampton Bays, NY*

PREP: 10 MIN. • COOK: 5 MIN./BATCH • MAKES: 4 SERVINGS

1 bunch kale, washed
2 Tbsp. olive oil
1 to 3 tsp. Old Bay Seasoning
Sea salt, to taste

1. Preheat air fryer to 375°. Remove tough stems from kale and tear leaves into large pieces. Place in a large bowl. Add olive oil and massage into leaves, coating evenly. Sprinkle kale with seasoning and salt. In batches, arrange leaves in a single layer on greased tray in air-fryer basket.

2. Cook until crisp and just starting to brown, 5-7 minutes. Let stand at least 5 minutes before serving.

1 serving: 101 cal., 7g fat (1g sat. fat), 0 chol., 202mg sod., 8g carb. (0 sugars, 2g fiber), 3g pro. **Diabetic exchanges:** 1½ fat, 1 vegetable.

AIR-FRYING TIP

Depending on the type of air fryer you're using, you may need only a light spritz of cooking spray on the bottom grate to help the food brown. However, if you find your food sticking, reapply the spray in between batches.

BUFFALO CHICKEN WINGS

Cayenne, red sauce and spices keep these tangy wings good and hot, just like the originals. The air fryer also keeps these wings on the healthier side.
—*Nancy Chapman, Center Harbor, NH*

PREP: 10 MIN. • COOK: 35 MIN./BATCH • MAKES: ABOUT 4 DOZEN

25 whole chicken wings
   (about 5 lbs.)
1 cup butter, cubed
¼ cup Louisiana-style
   hot sauce
¾ tsp. cayenne pepper
¾ tsp. celery salt
½ tsp. onion powder
½ tsp. garlic powder
   Optional: Celery ribs and
   ranch salad dressing

1. Preheat air fryer to 300°. Cut chicken wings into 3 sections; discard wing tip sections. In batches, arrange wings in a single layer on greased tray in air-fryer basket. Cook 15 minutes. Increase temperature to 400°; cook until chicken juices run clear and wings are golden brown, 20-25 minutes.

2. Meanwhile, in a small saucepan, melt butter. Stir in hot sauce and spices. Place chicken in a large bowl; add sauce and toss to coat. Remove to a serving plate with a slotted spoon. Serve with celery and ranch dressing if desired.

1 piece: 83 cal., 7g fat (3g sat. fat), 24mg chol., 106mg sod., 0 carb. (0 sugars, 0 fiber), 5g pro.

CRISPY CALAMARI

You can make crispy calamari just like your favorite Italian restaurant's version thanks to the air fryer! A quick coat in crunchy panko bread crumbs and a few minutes in the air fryer are all it takes to make this special appetizer.

—Peggy Woodward, Shullsburg, WI

PREP: 20 MIN. • COOK: 10 MIN./BATCH • MAKES: 5 DOZEN

½ cup all-purpose flour
½ tsp. salt
1 large egg, lightly beaten
½ cup 2% milk
1 cup panko bread crumbs
½ tsp. seasoned salt
¼ tsp. pepper
8 oz. cleaned fresh or frozen calamari (squid), thawed and cut into ½-in. rings
Cooking spray

1. Preheat air fryer to 400°. In a shallow bowl, combine flour and salt. In another shallow bowl, whisk egg and milk. In a third shallow bowl, combine bread crumbs, seasoned salt and pepper. Coat calamari with flour mixture, then dip in egg mixture and coat with bread crumb mixture.

2. In batches, place calamari in a single layer on greased tray in air-fryer basket; spritz with cooking spray. Cook 4 minutes. Turn; spritz with cooking spray. Cook calamari until golden brown, 3-5 minutes longer.

1 piece: 11 cal., 0 fat (0 sat. fat), 10mg chol., 28mg sod., 1g carb. (0 sugars, 0 fiber), 1g pro.

CHAPTER 2

BREAKFAST & BRUNCH

Take advantage of your air fryer for effortlessly easy morning meals. From fancy eggs, loaded potatoes and even sweet pastries, you'll have everything you need for a hot and cozy breakfast.

CINNAMON TEA ROLLS

By starting with refrigerated crescent roll dough, you can have fresh homemade cinnamon rolls in a few minutes. Using an air fryer makes it even easier!
—Taste of Home *Test Kitchen*

TAKES: 20 MIN. • MAKES: 4 ROLLS

1 tube (4 oz.) refrigerated crescent rolls
1 Tbsp. sugar
⅛ tsp. ground cinnamon
¼ cup confectioners' sugar
1¼ tsp. orange juice

1. Unroll crescent dough into 1 rectangle; seal perforations. Combine sugar and cinnamon; sprinkle over dough. Roll up jelly-roll style, starting with a short side; pinch seam to seal. Using a serrated knife, cut into 4 slices.

2. Preheat air fryer to 350°. Place rolls, pinched side down, in ungreased ramekins or individual silicone muffin cups. Place in air fryer. Cook until golden brown, 8-12 minutes. Cool for 5 minutes before removing from pan to a wire rack. In a small bowl, combine confectioners' sugar and orange juice; drizzle over rolls.

1 roll: 144 cal., 5g fat (2g sat. fat), 0 chol., 213mg sod., 23g carb. (14g sugars, 0 fiber), 2g pro.

AIR-FRYING TIP
To store, cool coffee cake completely. Place in an airtight container; keep at room temperature for 2–3 days.

RASPBERRY CRUMBLE COFFEE CAKE

With a ribbon of fresh homemade fruit filling, this homey coffee cake is perfect for breakfast with friends and family. It's equally delicious warm out of the air fryer for a weeknight dessert.
—*Shirley Royken, Mesa, AZ*

PREP: 25 MIN. • COOK: 30 MIN. • MAKES: 8 SERVINGS

FILLING
- ⅓ cup sugar
- 2 Tbsp. cornstarch
- 6 Tbsp. water or cranberry-raspberry juice
- 1 cup fresh or frozen unsweetened raspberries
- 1½ tsp. lemon juice

COFFEE CAKE
- 1½ cups all-purpose flour
- ½ cup sugar
- 1½ tsp. baking powder
- ½ tsp. salt
- ½ tsp. ground cinnamon
- ⅛ tsp. ground mace
- ½ cup cold butter, cubed
- 1 large egg, room temperature, lightly beaten
- ½ cup whole milk
- ½ tsp. vanilla extract

TOPPING
- 2 Tbsp. cold butter, cubed
- ¼ cup all-purpose flour
- ¼ cup sugar
- 2 Tbsp. sliced almonds

1. For filling, in a saucepan, combine sugar, cornstarch and water until smooth. Bring to a boil over medium heat. Cook and stir until thickened, 1-2 minutes. Add berries and lemon juice. Set aside to cool.

2. In a large bowl, combine flour, sugar, baking powder, salt, cinnamon and mace. Cut in butter to form fine crumbs. Stir in eggs, milk and vanilla until blended.

3. Spread half batter into a greased 8-in. round baking pan that fits into air fryer. Spread filling evenly over top. Drop remaining batter by small spoonfuls and spread evenly over filling.

4. Preheat air fryer to 325°. For topping, cut butter into flour and sugar; stir in almonds. Sprinkle over top. Place pan in air fryer; cook until a toothpick inserted in center comes out with moist crumbs and top is golden brown, 30-35 minutes.

1 piece: 376 cal., 17g fat (10g sat. fat), 63mg chol., 368mg sod., 53g carb. (29g sugars, 2g fiber), 5g pro.

SAUSAGE BACON BITES

Surprise your family on Sunday morning with these savory breakfast bites. They're equally delicious as a party appetizer. Get ready for oohs and aahs!
—*Pat Waymire, Yellow Springs, OH*

PREP: 20 MIN. + CHILLING • COOK: 15 MIN./BATCH • MAKES: ABOUT 3½ DOZEN

¾ lb. sliced bacon
2 pkg. (8 oz. each) frozen fully cooked breakfast sausage links, thawed
½ cup plus 2 Tbsp. packed brown sugar, divided

1. Cut bacon strips widthwise in half; cut sausage links in half. Wrap a piece of bacon around each piece of sausage. Place ½ cup brown sugar in a shallow bowl; roll sausages in sugar. Secure each with a toothpick. Place in a large bowl. Cover and refrigerate 4 hours or overnight.

2. Preheat air fryer to 325°. Sprinkle wrapped sausages with 1 Tbsp. brown sugar. In batches, arrange sausages in a single layer on greased tray in air-fryer basket. Cook until bacon is crisp, 15-20 minutes, turning once. Sprinkle with the remaining 1 Tbsp. brown sugar.

1 piece: 74 cal., 6g fat (2g sat. fat), 9mg chol., 154mg sod., 4g carb. (4g sugars, 0 fiber), 2g pro.

WHY YOU'LL LOVE IT...
"So delicious! I've made them a few times and everyone loves them. It is a very simple recipe—I was trying to think of something easy to make for a party and when I thought of these I knew they were perfect!"
—JULIASMOM, TASTEOFHOME.COM

BREAKFAST POTATOES

I frequently serve these potatoes for breakfast but they also make a wonderful side dish for dinner. Mix it up by swapping in a sweet potato or two.
—*Anita Osborne, Thomasburg, ON*

PREP: 20 MIN. • COOK: 30 MIN. • MAKES: 4 SERVINGS

6 garlic cloves, peeled
2 Tbsp. olive oil, divided
1 lb. potatoes, cut into ¼- to ½-in. cubes (about 3½ cups)
1 small sweet red pepper, cut into ½-in. pieces
½ tsp. salt
¼ tsp. pepper

1. Preheat air fryer to 400°. Cut stem ends off unpeeled garlic cloves. Place cloves on a piece of foil. Drizzle with 1 Tbsp. oil; wrap in foil. Place in air fryer. Cook until cloves are soft, 15-20 minutes. Unwrap and cool 10 minutes.

2. Meanwhile, in a large bowl, toss potatoes, red pepper, salt, pepper and remaining 1 Tbsp. oil. Transfer mixture to greased tray in air-fryer basket. Cook, stirring occasionally, until potatoes are tender, 12-15 minutes. Stir in reserved garlic.

¾ cup: 160 cal., 7g fat (1g sat. fat), 0 chol., 303mg sod., 23g carb. (2g sugars, 3g fiber), 3g pro. **Diabetic exchanges:** 1½ starch, 1 fat.

HARD-BOILED EGGS

Here's an alternate method to boiling eggs on the stovetop.
These air-fried eggs are just as easy and super quick!
—*Rashanda Cobbins, Milwaukee, WI*

TAKES: 25 MIN. + CHILLING • MAKES: 6 SERVINGS

6   large eggs

Preheat air fryer to 275°. Place eggs in a single layer on tray in air fryer basket. Cook 15 minutes. Remove eggs; rinse in cold water and place in ice water until completely cooled. Drain and refrigerate. Remove shells; if desired, cut eggs before serving.

1 egg: 72 cal., 5g fat (2g sat. fat), 186mg chol., 71mg sod., 0 carb. (0 sugars, 0 fiber), 6g pro. **Diabetic exchanges:** 1 medium-fat meat.

TEST KITCHEN TIP: Older eggs are best for hard-boiling. Eggs that are close to their best-by date will peel much easier than fresh eggs. It's also best to remove your eggs from the fridge at least 30 minutes before you plan to cook them. This will help them cook evenly and prevent the shell from cracking.

BANANA BREAD

Yes, you can make banana bread in the air fryer! This easy recipe is a cinch to put together. Eat it while it's still warm or at room temperature with a schmear of butter.
—*Peggy Woodward, Shullsburg, WI*

PREP: 10 MIN. • COOK: 25 MIN. + COOLING • MAKES: 8 SERVINGS

- ¼ cup butter, softened
- ¾ cup sugar
- 1 large egg, room temperature
- 1 cup all-purpose flour
- ½ tsp. baking soda
- ¼ tsp. salt
- ⅔ cup mashed ripe banana (about 1 medium)
- ½ cup chopped pecans

1. Preheat air fryer to 325°. In a large bowl, cream butter and sugar until light and fluffy, 3-4 minutes. Beat in egg. In another bowl, whisk flour, baking soda and salt; add to creamed mixture alternately with banana, beating well after each addition. Fold in pecans.

2. Transfer to a greased 8-in. round baking pan that will fit in the air fryer. Cook until a toothpick inserted in center comes out clean, 20-25 minutes. Cover tightly with foil if top gets too dark. Cool in pan on a wire rack for 10 minutes before removing from the pan.

1 piece: 254 cal., 11g fat (4g sat. fat), 39mg chol., 208mg sod., 36g carb. (22g sugars, 2g fiber), 3g pro.

CINNAMON DOUGHNUTS

My sons and I love doughnuts, but in the Florida heat, I rarely want to deep-fry them. I made this easy version in my air fryer, and it turned out so well with no mess!
—*Christine Hair, Odessa, FL*

TAKES: 25 MIN. • MAKES: 8 DOUGHNUTS + 8 DOUGHNUT HOLES

1 tube (16.3 oz.) large refrigerated buttermilk biscuits (8 count)
¾ cup sugar
2 tsp. ground cinnamon
¼ cup butter, melted
1 tsp. vanilla extract

1. Preheat air fryer to 375°. Separate biscuits. Cut out centers using a 1-in. cutter; save centers. In batches, place doughnuts in a single layer on greased tray in air-fryer basket. Cook until golden brown and puffed, turning once, about 5 minutes. In batches, cook doughnut holes until golden brown, 3-4 minutes.

2. Meanwhile, in a shallow dish, combine sugar and cinnamon. In a separate bowl, mix melted butter and vanilla. Brush doughnuts and doughnut holes with butter; toss in sugar mixture. Serve doughnuts warm.

1 doughnut and 1 doughnut hole: 280 cal., 15g fat (8g sat. fat), 23mg chol., 684mg sod., 33g carb. (11g sugars, 1g fiber), 4g pro.

SAVORY SAUSAGE PATTIES

These patties are quick to prepare on a moment's notice, but you can also mix up a couple of batches and have them ready to go in the freezer. Just pop them in the air fryer for about 10 minutes and breakfast is ready!

—Carole Thomson, Komarno, MB

TAKES: 20 MIN. • MAKES: 6 SERVINGS

1 large egg, beaten
⅓ cup milk
½ cup chopped onion
2 Tbsp. all-purpose flour
⅛ tsp. salt
  Dash pepper
1 lb. sage bulk pork sausage

1. Preheat air fryer to 400°. In a large bowl, combine the first 6 ingredients. Crumble sausage over mixture and mix lightly but thoroughly. Shape into 6 patties.

2. Place patties in a single layer on greased tray in air-fryer basket. Cook until the meat is no longer pink, 8-10 minutes, turning once.

Freeze option: Prepare uncooked patties and freeze, covered, on a foil-lined baking sheet until firm. Transfer patties to a freezer container; return to the freezer. To use, cook the frozen patties as directed, increasing the time as necessary for a thermometer to read 160°.

1 patty: 219 cal., 18g fat (6g sat. fat), 73mg chol., 527mg sod., 5g carb. (1g sugars, 0 fiber), 10g pro.

LOADED HASH BROWNS

These hash browns are one of my go-to sides. They come together quickly, and the air fryer gets them nice and crispy in no time. If you like, top them with a sprinkling of shredded pepper jack cheese.
—*Cindi Boger, Ardmore, AL*

PREP: 20 MIN. • COOK: 15 MIN./BATCH • MAKES: 12 SERVINGS

1 pkg. (30 oz.) frozen shredded hash brown potatoes
1 large red onion, finely chopped
1 small sweet red pepper, finely chopped
1 small green pepper, finely chopped
4 garlic cloves, minced
2 Tbsp. olive oil
½ tsp. salt
½ tsp. pepper
3 drops hot pepper sauce, optional
2 tsp. minced fresh parsley

Preheat air fryer to 375°. In a large bowl, combine the first 8 ingredients; if desired, add hot sauce. In batches, spread mixture in an even ¾-in.-thick layer in greased tray in air-fryer basket. Cook until golden and crispy, 15-20 minutes. Sprinkle with parsley just before serving.

½ cup: 87 cal., 2g fat (0 sat. fat), 0 chol., 116mg sod., 15g carb. (2g sugars, 2g fiber), 2g pro. **Diabetic exchanges:** 1 starch, ½ fat.

AIR-FRYING TIP

Preheat the air fryer for about 5 minutes before adding the hash browns. This will allow the hash browns to start cooking immediately instead of sitting cold while the air fryer heats up.

HOMEMADE BREAKFAST BITES

These scrumptious breakfast treats are so quick and easy to make in the
air fryer. The crispy sugar coating is hard to resist.

—*Ruth Hastings, Louisville, IL*

PREP: 15 MIN. • COOK: 10 MIN./BATCH • MAKES: 6 SERVINGS (1½ DOZEN)

1⅓ cups all-purpose flour
1 cup crisp rice cereal,
  coarsely crushed
2 Tbsp. plus ½ cup
  sugar, divided
1 Tbsp. baking powder
½ tsp. salt
¼ cup butter-flavored
  shortening
½ cup 2% milk
1 tsp. ground cinnamon
¼ cup butter, melted

1. In a large bowl, combine flour, cereal, 2 Tbsp. sugar, baking powder and salt; cut in shortening until the mixture resembles coarse crumbs. Stir in milk just until moistened. Shape into 1-in. balls.

2. Preheat the air fryer to 400°. In a shallow bowl, combine the remaining ½ cup sugar and cinnamon. Dip balls in butter, then roll in cinnamon-sugar.

3. In batches, arrange in a single layer on greased tray in air-fryer basket. Cook until browned and a toothpick inserted in centers comes out clean, 8-12 minutes.

3 balls: 355 cal., 17g fat (7g sat. fat), 22mg chol., 533mg sod., 48g carb. (23g sugars, 1g fiber), 4g pro.

TEST KITCHEN TIP: These breakfast bites are similar to traditional doughnut holes. You can exchange the cinnamon-sugar coating for powdered sugar if you like. Omit rolling the balls in the cinnamon and sugar prior to air frying. After they are done baking in the air fryer, and while they are still warm, roll the balls in powdered sugar before they cool off completely (the sugar sticks better this way).

HONEY-COCONUT STICKY BUNS

There's nothing better than a warm sticky bun on a chilly morning,
or any morning for that matter. Hot out of the air fryer, dripping with
butter-honey and loaded with coconut, these treats are pure heaven!
—*Diane Nemitz, Ludington, MI*

PREP: 20 MIN. + RISING • COOK: 20 MIN./BATCH • MAKES: 16 SERVINGS

1 loaf (1 lb.) frozen bread
  dough, thawed
4 oz. (½ cup) cream
  cheese, softened
½ cup sweetened
  shredded coconut
3 Tbsp. thawed orange
  juice concentrate
½ cup butter
½ cup honey
  Optional: Toasted
  sweetened shredded
  coconut and grated
  orange zest

1. Grease two 8-in. round baking pans that fit in air fryer. Cut thawed bread dough in half; roll each half into a 10x8-in. rectangle. Combine cream cheese, coconut and orange juice concentrate; spread mixture on dough. Roll up jelly-roll style, starting with long side. Cut each roll crosswise into 8 slices; place in prepared pans. Cover; let rise until almost doubled, about 1 hour.

2. Preheat air fryer to 325°. In a microwave, melt butter and honey. Spoon 1 Tbsp. butter-honey mixture over each bun. In batches, place pans in air fryer; cook until tops are golden brown, about 20 minutes. Immediately invert onto a serving plate. If desired, top with toasted coconut and orange zest.

1 bun: 206 cal., 10g fat (6g sat. fat), 22mg chol., 235mg sod., 25g carb. (12g sugars, 1g fiber), 4g pro.

EGGS LORRAINE

Whenever I'm looking to impress overnight guests at breakfast, this is the recipe I serve. It's easy to assemble and cooks quickly in the air fryer.
—*Sandra Woolard, DeLand, FL*

TAKES: 25 MIN. • MAKES: 2 SERVINGS

4   slices Canadian bacon
2   slices Swiss cheese
4   large eggs
2   Tbsp. sour cream
⅛   tsp. salt
⅛   tsp. pepper
    Minced chives, optional

1. Preheat air fryer to 325°. Coat 2 shallow oval 1½-cup baking dishes that fit in air fryer with cooking spray. Line with Canadian bacon; top with cheese. Carefully break 2 eggs into each dish.

2. In a small bowl, whisk the sour cream, salt and pepper until smooth; drop by teaspoonfuls onto eggs. Place dishes in the air fryer. Cook until eggs are set, 10-15 minutes. If desired, sprinkle with chives.

1 serving: 258 cal., 18g fat (7g sat. fat), 406mg chol., 687mg sod., 2g carb. (1g sugars, 0 fiber), 22g pro.

WHY YOU'LL LOVE IT...
"I served it atop pieces of warm sourdough bread after baking. Delicious and very hearty. Will make this again!"
—ANNRMS, TASTEOFHOME.COM

TAHITIAN BREAKFAST TREATS

In Tahiti, people often enjoy firi firi—light and airy coconut pastries similar
to a doughnut—for breakfast. They're traditionally deep-fried,
but they come out just as delicious in my air fryer.
—*Susan Falk, Sterling Heights, MI*

PREP: 35 MIN. + RISING • COOK: 10 MIN./BATCH • MAKES: 8 SERVINGS

¼ cup warm water
    (110° to 115°)
1 pkg. (¼ oz.) active dry yeast
½ cup warm coconut
    milk (110° to 115°)
½ cup sweetened
    shredded coconut
⅓ cup sugar
½ tsp. salt
2 to 2½ cups all-purpose flour

SPICED SUGAR

½ cup sugar
1 tsp. ground cinnamon
½ tsp. ground ginger
½ vanilla bean
¼ cup butter, melted

AIR-FRYING TIP
These breakfast pastries would be even more delicious with a glaze drizzled on top. Combine 1 cup powdered sugar, 3 Tbsp. dark rum and 2 Tbsp. melted butter. Lightly drizzle over warm pastries.

1. Add yeast to warm water and stir to dissolve; allow to sit until yeast has bubbled, 5-7 minutes. Add the yeast mixture to warm coconut milk. In a large bowl, combine coconut, sugar, salt, yeast mixture and 1 cup flour; beat on medium speed until smooth. Stir in enough remaining flour to form a stiff dough (dough will be sticky). Turn dough onto a floured surface; knead until smooth and elastic, 6-8 minutes. Place dough in a greased bowl, turning once to grease the top. Cover and let rise in a warm place until doubled, about 1½ hours.

2. Punch down dough. Turn onto a lightly floured surface; divide into 8 portions. Roll each into a 12-in. rope. Curl ends in opposite directions to form a figure 8. Tuck each end under where it meets center of roll and pinch lightly to seal. Place 2 in. apart on a parchment-lined baking sheet. Cover with a kitchen towel; let rise in a warm place until almost doubled, about 30 minutes.

3. Preheat air fryer to 325°. In batches, arrange in a single layer on a greased tray in air-fryer basket. Cook until light brown, 7-10 minutes. Meanwhile, place sugar, cinnamon and ginger in a shallow bowl. Split the vanilla bean lengthwise. Using the tip of a sharp knife, scrape seeds from the center; stir into sugar mixture. Brush warm pastries with melted butter; roll in sugar mixture to coat.

1 pastry: 251 cal., 8g fat (6g sat. fat), 8mg chol., 191mg sod., 42g carb. (18g sugars, 1g fiber), 4g pro.

CHAPTER 3

SIDE DISHES

The main dish may be the star, but it's the stellar sides that make the meal. From crispy potatoes to herb-roasted veggies, these air-fried sides will round out menus without all the extra oil.

STUFFED SWEET POTATOES

These stuffed sweet potatoes make a perfect holiday side dish.
To save time, prepare them in the morning, then refrigerate after stuffing.
Finish baking them in the air fryer just before serving.
—Joan Hallford, North Richland Hills, TX

PREP: 20 MIN. • COOK: 45 MIN. • MAKES: 4 SERVINGS

2 medium sweet potatoes
1 tsp. olive oil
1 cup cooked chopped spinach, drained
1 cup shredded cheddar cheese, divided
2 cooked bacon strips, crumbled
1 green onion, chopped
¼ cup fresh cranberries, coarsely chopped
⅓ cup chopped pecans, toasted
2 Tbsp. butter
¼ tsp. kosher salt
¼ tsp. pepper

1. Preheat air fryer to 400°. Brush potatoes with oil. Place on tray in air-fryer basket. Cook until the potatoes are tender, 30-40 minutes; cool slightly.

2. Cut potatoes in half lengthwise. Scoop out pulp, leaving a ¼-in.-thick shell. In a large bowl, mash the potato pulp; stir in spinach, ¾ cup cheese, bacon, onion, cranberries, pecans, butter, salt and pepper. Spoon into potato shells, mounding mixture slightly.

3. Reduce heat to 360°. Place potato halves, cut side up, on tray in air-fryer basket. Cook 10 minutes. Sprinkle with remaining ¼ cup cheese; cook until cheese is melted, 1-2 minutes.

1 stuffed potato half: 376 cal., 25g fat (10g sat. fat), 49mg chol., 489mg sod., 28g carb. (10g sugars, 5g fiber), 12g pro.

GARLIC BREAD

Don't heat up the oven when you're craving garlic bread. Instead,
use your air fryer to make perfectly toasted bread that's done in a flash.
I use fresh garlic, but ½ teaspoon garlic powder also will work.
—*Peggy Woodward, Shullsburg, WI*

TAKES: 20 MIN. • MAKES: 8 SERVINGS

¼ cup butter, softened
3 Tbsp. grated
  Parmesan cheese
2 garlic cloves, minced
2 tsp. minced fresh parsley or
  ½ tsp. dried parsley flakes
8 slices ciabatta or
  French bread

1. Preheat air fryer to 350°. In a small bowl, combine the first
4 ingredients; spread over bread.

2. In batches, arrange bread in a single layer on tray in air-fryer
basket. Cook until golden brown, 2-3 minutes. Serve warm.

1 piece: 122 cal., 7g fat (4g sat. fat), 17mg chol., 181mg sod., 14g carb. (1g sugars, 1g fiber),
3g pro.

GINGER BUTTERNUT SQUASH

Coating butternut squash in a tart orange glaze gives this side dish a unique
and surprising flavor. Low in fat and sodium, it comes together fast so you
can spend less time in the kitchen and more time with family.
—Taste of Home *Test Kitchen*

PREP: 15 MIN. • COOK: 20 MIN. • MAKES: 5 SERVINGS

1 butternut squash
  (2 lbs.), peeled and cut
  into 1½-in. cubes
½ cup thawed orange
  juice concentrate
4 tsp. coarsely chopped
  fresh gingerroot
¼ tsp. pepper
2 tsp. butter, melted

Preheat air fryer to 375°. In a large bowl, toss squash, orange
juice concentrate, ginger and pepper. Transfer to greased tray
in air-fryer basket. Cook until squash is tender, 20-25 minutes,
stirring every 5 minutes. Stir in butter before serving.

½ cup: 136 cal., 2g fat (1g sat. fat), 4mg chol., 22mg sod., 31g carb. (13g sugars, 6g fiber),
3g pro. **Diabetic exchanges:** 1 starch, 1 fruit, ½ fat.

TEST KITCHEN TIP: Feel free to add a touch of garlic powder,
rosemary or paprika to this recipe. Or, for a sweeter version, use
cinnamon and brown sugar to season your squash.

CABBAGE & ONIONS

You'll be amazed how the air fryer brings out the sweetness of the cabbage and onions. The vinegar-mustard sauce makes this dish similar to a warm slaw.
—*Ann Sheehy, Lawrence, MA*

PREP: 10 MIN. • COOK: 15 MIN. + STANDING • MAKES: 6 SERVINGS

1   medium head cabbage (about 2 lbs.), coarsely chopped
2   large onions, chopped
¼   cup olive oil
¾   tsp. salt
¾   tsp. pepper
3   Tbsp. minced fresh chives
3   Tbsp. minced fresh tarragon

DRESSING
2   Tbsp. white balsamic vinegar or white wine vinegar
2   Tbsp. olive oil
2   Tbsp. Dijon mustard
1   Tbsp. lemon juice
½   tsp. salt
½   tsp. pepper

1. Preheat air fryer to 400°. Place cabbage and onions in a large bowl. Drizzle with oil; sprinkle with salt and pepper and toss to coat. In batches, place cabbage on greased tray in air-fryer basket. Cook until vegetables are tender and lightly browned, 12-15 minutes, stirring halfway through.

2. Transfer cabbage mixture to a large bowl. Add chives and tarragon; toss to combine. In a small bowl, whisk the dressing ingredients until blended. Drizzle over cabbage mixture; toss to coat. Let stand 10 minutes to allow flavors to blend. Serve warm or at room temperature.

¾ cup: 183 cal., 14g fat (2g sat. fat), 0 chol., 636mg sod., 14g carb. (7g sugars, 4g fiber), 2g pro.

WHY YOU'LL LOVE IT...
"This is a great recipe, both for taste and ease of preparing. Also a novel idea that is growing more and more popular of using vinaigrette on veggies. Hubby and I love it!"
—JANESMITH, TASTEOFHOME.COM

ZUCCHINI FRIES

When I make burgers and sandwiches, I serve them with these
zucchini strips instead of french fries. They're crispy and delicious
and a great way to use up the zucchini in my garden.
—*Matthew Hass, Ellison Bay, WI*

PREP: 25 MIN. • COOK: 15 MIN./BATCH • MAKES: 4 SERVINGS

2   medium zucchini
1   cup panko bread crumbs
¾   cup grated Parmesan
    cheese
2   tsp. smoked paprika
½   tsp. garlic powder
¼   tsp. ground chipotle pepper
¼   tsp. salt
¼   tsp. pepper
⅓   cup all-purpose flour
2   large eggs, beaten
    Cooking spray

1. Preheat air fryer to 400°. Cut each zucchini in half lengthwise
and then cut in half crosswise. Cut each piece lengthwise into
¼-in. slices.

2. In a shallow bowl, mix bread crumbs, cheese and seasonings.
Place flour and eggs in separate shallow bowls. Dip zucchini
slices in flour, then in egg and then in crumb mixture, patting
to help coating adhere.

3. In batches, place zucchini on greased tray in air-fryer basket;
spritz with cooking spray. Cook until fries are golden brown,
15-20 minutes, stirring every 5 minutes, .

1 serving: 207 cal., 8g fat (3g sat. fat), 106mg chol., 510mg sod., 22g carb. (3g sugars,
2g fiber), 12g pro.

LEMON PEPPER BROCCOLI

I'm convinced broccoli was made to be cooked in an air fryer. It cooks up tender but still has a nice crunch. It gets even better with a touch of lemon!
—*Liz Bellville, Tonasket, WA*

TAKES: 25 MIN. • MAKES: 8 SERVINGS

2   Tbsp. olive oil
½   tsp. lemon juice
¼   tsp. salt
¼   tsp. coarsely ground pepper, divided
1½ lbs. fresh broccoli florets (about 12 cups)
¼   cup chopped almonds
2   tsp. grated lemon zest
    Lemon wedges, optional

1. Preheat air fryer to 400°. In a large bowl, whisk the oil, lemon juice, salt and ⅛ tsp. pepper until blended; add broccoli and toss to coat. Arrange broccoli in a single layer on greased tray in air-fryer basket.

2. Cook until tender, 8-10 minutes. Transfer to a serving dish. Sprinkle with almonds, lemon zest and remaining ⅛ tsp. pepper; toss to combine. If desired, serve with lemon wedges.

1 cup: 84 cal., 6g fat (1g sat. fat), 0 chol., 103mg sod., 6g carb. (2g sugars, 3g fiber), 4g pro. **Diabetic exchanges:** 1 vegetable, 1 fat.

AIR-FRYING TIP

Toss in shaved Parmesan cheese for added richness, or add a light drizzle of balsamic glaze for a flavor punch.

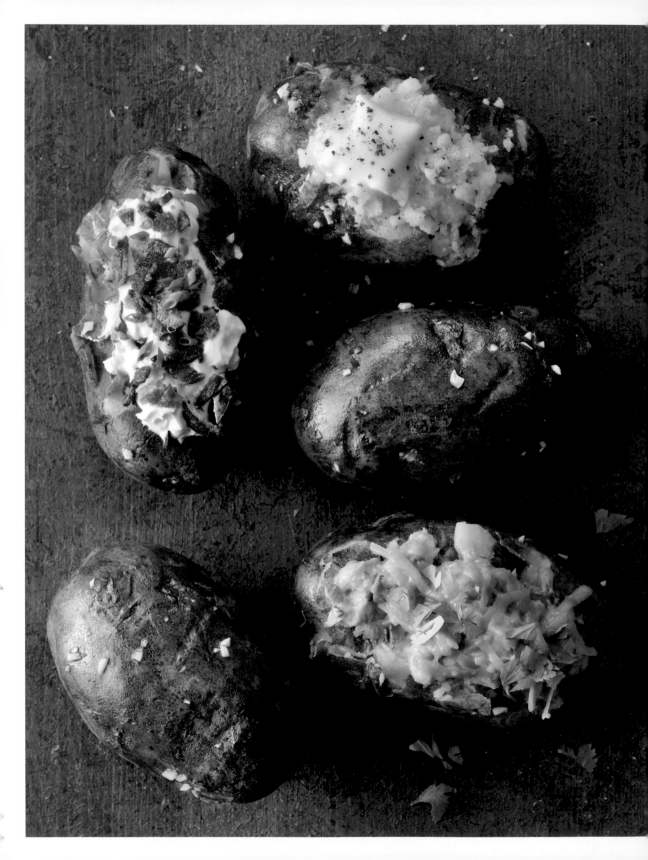

BAKED POTATOES

Upgrade standard baked potatoes by rubbing their skins with a flavorful butter-garlic mixture. It's a little extra incentive to eat the best part of the potato.
—*Teresa Emrick, Tipp City, OH*

PREP: 10 MIN. • COOK: 35 MIN. • MAKES: 4 SERVINGS

4   medium russet potatoes
2   Tbsp. butter, softened
2   garlic cloves, minced
¼   tsp. salt
¼   tsp. pepper
     Optional: Sour cream, butter, crumbled bacon, minced chives, guacamole, shredded cheddar cheese and minced fresh cilantro

1. Preheat air fryer to 400°. Scrub potatoes; pierce each several times with a fork. In a small bowl, mix butter, garlic, salt and pepper. Rub potatoes with butter mixture. Wrap each tightly in a piece of foil.

2. Place potatoes in a single layer on tray in air-fryer basket. Cook until fork tender, 35-45 minutes, rotating halfway through.

1 potato: 217 cal., 6g fat (4g sat. fat), 15mg chol., 206mg sod., 38g carb. (2g sugars, 5g fiber), 5g pro.

SEASONED PLANTAINS

Having grown up in Puerto Rico, I've had the opportunity to try many great Caribbean foods. Tostones—crispy, fried green plaintains—rank among my favorites. This air-fried version has the same great taste as traditional deep-fried but with fewer calories.
—*Leah Martin, Gilbertsville, PA*

PREP: 15 MIN. + SOAKING • COOK: 15 MIN./BATCH • MAKES: 3 DOZEN

3 garlic cloves, minced
1 Tbsp. garlic salt
½ tsp. onion powder
6 green plantains, peeled and cut into 1-in. slices
Cooking spray

SEASONING MIX
1 Tbsp. garlic powder
1½ tsp. garlic salt
½ tsp. onion powder
½ tsp. kosher salt
Optional: Guacamole and pico de gallo

1. In a large bowl, combine garlic, garlic salt and onion powder. Add plantains; cover with cold water. Soak for 30 minutes. Drain plantains; place on paper towels and pat dry.

2. Preheat air fryer to 375°. In batches, place plantains in a single layer on greased tray in air-fryer basket; spritz with cooking spray. Cook until lightly browned, 10-12 minutes. Place plantain pieces between 2 sheets of aluminum foil. With the bottom of a glass, flatten to ½-in. thickness. Increase air-fryer temperature to 400°. Return flattened plantains to air fryer; cook until golden brown, 2-3 minutes longer. Combine seasoning mix ingredients; sprinkle over tostones.

1 tostone: 39 cal., 0 fat (0 sat. fat), 0 chol., 110mg sod., 10g carb. (4g sugars, 1g fiber), 0 pro.

AIR-FRYING TIP
No baby carrots on hand? This recipe also works with regular carrots peeled and cut into 2-in. sections. They may take a few minutes longer to cook thoroughly in the air fryer. Pierce with a fork to check for tenderness.

THYME-ROASTED CARROTS

Roasting carrots brings out their sweetness. Thyme complements their flavor, but feel free to mix it up and use other herbs such as rosemary or tarragon.
—*Marlene Schott, Devine, TX*

TAKES: 30 MIN. • MAKES: 4 SERVINGS

1 lb. baby carrots
2 small onions, quartered
3 garlic cloves, peeled
1 Tbsp. olive oil
1 tsp. white wine vinegar
1 tsp. dried thyme
¼ tsp. salt
⅛ tsp. pepper
  Fresh thyme, optional

Preheat air fryer to 375°. In a large bowl, toss first 8 ingredients. Place carrots on greased tray in air-fryer basket. Cook until carrots are crisp-tender, 18-20 minutes, stirring occasionally. If desired, sprinkle with fresh thyme.

¾ **cup:** 88 cal., 3g fat (0 sat. fat), 0 chol., 230mg sod., 15g carb. (7g sugars, 3g fiber), 2g pro. **Diabetic exchanges:** 2 vegetable, ½ fat.

GARLIC CORN ON THE COB

In the summer, there's nothing better than fresh corn on the cob.
I've loved it served with this seasoning blend since I was a kid.
—Anna Minegar, Zolfo Springs, FL

TAKES: 30 MIN. • MAKES: 4 SERVINGS

4 medium ears sweet
  corn, husked
2 Tbsp. butter, melted
1½ tsp. dried parsley flakes
1½ tsp. garlic pepper blend
¼ tsp. paprika
⅛ tsp. salt

1. Preheat air fryer to 375°. Brush corn with half the butter; place on tray in air-fryer basket. Cook until tender and starting to brown, 12-15 minutes.

2. Meanwhile, in a small bowl, combine parsley, garlic pepper, paprika and salt. Brush corn with remaining butter; sprinkle with seasoning mixture.

1 ear of corn: 140 cal., 7g fat (4g sat. fat), 15mg chol., 241mg sod., 19g carb. (6g sugars, 2g fiber), 3g pro. **Diabetic exchanges:** 1½ fat, 1 starch.

ONION CRESCENT ROLLS

French-fried onions aren't just for green bean casserole.
Sprinkle them onto crescent roll dough before rolling up and
you'll end up with a crunchy treat inside flaky pastry.
—*Barbara Nowakowski, North Tonawanda, NY*

TAKES: 20 MIN. • MAKES: 8 SERVINGS

1 tube (8 oz.) refrigerated crescent rolls
1⅓ cups french-fried onions, divided
1 large egg
1 Tbsp. water

1. Do not preheat air fryer. Unroll crescent dough and separate into triangles. Sprinkle each with about 2 Tbsp. onions. Roll up each from the wide end. Curve ends down to form crescents.

2. In batches, place crescents in a single layer on greased tray in air-fryer basket. Beat egg and water; brush over dough. Sprinkle with the remaining onions. Cook at 325° until golden brown, 7-8 minutes. Serve warm.

1 roll: 170 cal., 10g fat (4g sat. fat), 23mg chol., 301mg sod., 16g carb. (3g sugars, 0 fiber), 3g pro.

GARLICKY POTATO LATKES

Hot, crispy potato latkes are such a treat, but who wants to deal
with all the oil and grease? I tried making them in an air fryer
and they came out just as good—without all the cleanup!
—*Nancy Salinas, Grand Rapids, MN*

PREP: 20 MIN. • COOK: 15 MIN./BATCH • MAKES: 3 SERVINGS

2 medium potatoes, peeled
1 large egg
⅓ cup chopped onion
1 Tbsp. all-purpose flour
½ tsp. salt
¼ tsp. pepper
¼ tsp. garlic powder
   Cooking spray

1. Finely grate potatoes; firmly squeeze and drain any liquid.
Place potatoes in a large bowl. Add the egg, onion, flour, salt,
pepper and garlic powder; mix well.

2. Preheat air fryer to 375°. In batches, drop the batter by
¼ cupfuls onto greased tray in air-fryer basket; press lightly
to flatten. Spritz with cooking spray. Cook until golden brown,
12-17 minutes. Serve immediately.

2 latkes: 134 cal., 3g fat (1g sat. fat), 62mg chol., 421mg sod., 24g carb. (2g sugars,
2g fiber), 4g pro. **Diabetic exchanges:** 1½ starch.

AIR-FRYING TIP

A quick return to the air fryer for 3-4 minutes will bring leftover latkes back to a lovely crisp state.

BRUSSELS SPROUTS WITH BACON

Different air fryers cook at different speeds, so keep an eye on these so they don't get too crisp. The bacon may need to precook a little more if you get thicker bacon slices.
—*Karen Keefe, Phoenix, AZ*

PREP: 10 MIN. • COOK: 20 MIN. • MAKES: 6 SERVINGS

6   bacon strips
2   lbs. Brussels
     sprouts, halved
2   Tbsp. olive oil
½   tsp. kosher salt
½   tsp. pepper
2   Tbsp. balsamic glaze

1. Preheat air fryer to 400°. Arrange bacon in a single layer on greased tray in air-fryer basket. Cook until partially cooked, 6-8 minutes, turning halfway through. Remove; coarsely chop. Wipe out air fryer.

2. In a large bowl, toss Brussels sprouts, bacon, olive oil, salt and pepper. In batches, place Brussels sprouts in a single layer on tray in air-fryer basket. Cook, stirring halfway through, until the sprouts are tender and lightly browned, 10-15 minutes. Drizzle with balsamic glaze; serve warm.

¾ **cup:** 227 cal., 16g fat (4g sat. fat), 18mg chol., 381mg sod., 16g carb. (5g sugars, 5g fiber), 8g pro.

HONEY SWEET POTATOES

The flavors of sweet potatoes, cinnamon and honey are classics.
Try this side dish with roast chicken or pork.

—Laura Mifsud, Northville, MI

PREP: 10 MIN. • COOK: 20 MIN. • MAKES: 6 SERVINGS

3 Tbsp. honey
2 Tbsp. olive oil
¾ tsp. ground cinnamon
½ tsp. salt
¼ tsp. pepper
3 medium sweet potatoes, peeled and cut into ½-in. cubes

Preheat air fryer to 350°. In a large bowl, whisk together honey, oil, cinnamon, salt and pepper; add potatoes and toss to coat. Transfer to greased tray in air-fryer basket. Cook until potatoes are tender, 20-25 minutes, stirring every 5 minutes.

¾ cup: 169 cal., 5g fat (1g sat. fat), 0 chol., 207mg sod., 32g carb. (18g sugars, 3g fiber), 2g pro. **Diabetic exchanges:** 2 starch, ½ fat.

TEST KITCHEN TIP: Before prepping the recipe, store the sweet potatoes in a cool, dry place such as a pantry. Don't store them in the refrigerator, as this will make the centers hard, and the flavor will not be as pleasant once cooked.

PARMESAN POTATO WEDGES

I love using the air fryer for these potato wedges because the outside gets golden brown and crispy while the interior stays fluffy and tender. Try serving them with steak, roasts or even burgers.

—*Linda Rock, Stratford, WI*

PREP: 10 MIN. • COOK: 15 MIN. • MAKES: 6 SERVINGS

4 russet potatoes (about 2 lbs.)
2 tsp. canola oil
½ cup grated Parmesan cheese
1 tsp. dried basil
1 tsp. seasoned salt
¼ tsp. onion powder
¼ tsp. garlic powder
¼ tsp. pepper

1. Preheat air fryer to 400°. Cut each potato lengthwise in half. Cut each half into 3 wedges. In a large bowl, drizzle potatoes with oil; toss to coat. Combine the remaining ingredients. Add to potatoes; toss to coat.

2. In batches, arrange potatoes in a single layer on greased tray in air-fryer basket. Cook until potato wedges are golden brown and tender, 15-20 minutes.

4 wedges: 152 cal., 4g fat (1g sat. fat), 6mg chol., 382mg sod., 26g carb. (1g sugars, 3g fiber), 5g pro. **Diabetic exchanges:** 2 starch, ½ fat.

WHY YOU'LL LOVE IT...
"These were amazing! I added just a touch of chili powder for a little kick."
—CBENNE12, TASTEOFHOME.COM

BUFFALO CAULIFLOWER

I love Buffalo wings, but sometimes I'm looking for something a little different.
Enter cauliflower! This is great as an appetizer or as a side dish.
—*Emily Tyra, Lake Ann, MI*

TAKES: 20 MIN. • MAKES: 8 SERVINGS

1 medium head cauliflower (about 2¼ lbs.), cut into florets
1 Tbsp. canola oil
½ cup Buffalo wing sauce
Blue cheese salad dressing

1. Preheat air fryer to 400°. Toss cauliflower with oil. Place in a single layer on tray in air-fryer basket. Cook until tender and lightly browned, 15-20 minutes, stirring halfway through.

2. Transfer to a serving bowl; toss with wing sauce. Serve with dressing.

⅓ **cup:** 39 cal., 2g fat (0 sat. fat), 0 chol., 474mg sod., 5g carb. (2g sugars, 2g fiber), 2g pro.

BALSAMIC ZUCCHINI

When your garden is producing an abundance of zucchini, it's time to pull out your air fryer. The handy appliance cooks sliced zucchini quickly and deliciously.
—*Joe Cherry, Metuchen, NJ*

TAKES: 15 MIN. • MAKES: 4 SERVINGS

3 medium zucchini, cut into ½-in. slices
2 garlic cloves, minced
1 Tbsp. olive oil
¼ tsp. salt
¼ cup balsamic vinegar

1. Preheat air fryer to 400°. In a large bowl, toss zucchini, garlic, oil and salt. Arrange zucchini in a single layer on tray in air-fryer basket. Cook until tender and golden brown, 7-10 minutes.

2. Meanwhile, in a small saucepan, bring the vinegar to a boil. Reduce heat and simmer until reduced by half. Place zucchini in a serving bowl; drizzle with vinegar. Toss to coat.

⅔ **cup:** 72 cal., 4g fat (1g sat. fat), 0 chol., 160mg sod., 9g carb. (7g sugars, 1g fiber), 2g pro. **Diabetic exchanges:** 1 vegetable, 1 fat.

TWICE-BAKED POTATO

Roasting garlic mellows out the flavor nicely but also changes it to create a sweet yet savory tone that's ideal for a twice-baked potato. I bake and stuff the potato halves ahead and then cook them the second time just before it's time to eat. Increase the second cook time as needed until they're heated through.
—*Nancy Mueller, Menomonee Falls, WI*

PREP: 20 MIN. • COOK: 40 MIN. • MAKES: 2 SERVINGS

1 large baking potato
1 tsp. canola oil, divided
6 garlic cloves, unpeeled
2 Tbsp. butter, softened
2 Tbsp. 2% milk
2 Tbsp. sour cream
¼ tsp. minced fresh rosemary or dash dried rosemary, crushed
⅛ tsp. salt
⅛ tsp. pepper

1. Preheat air fryer to 400°. Scrub and pierce potato; rub with ½ tsp. oil. Place garlic on a sheet of aluminum foil; drizzle with remaining ½ tsp. oil. Place potato and garlic on tray in air-fryer basket. Cook 15 minutes. Remove garlic; cook potato until tender, 20-25 minutes longer.

2. When cool enough to handle, cut potato in half lengthwise. Scoop out the pulp, leaving thin shells.

3. Squeeze softened garlic into a small bowl; add potato pulp and mash. Stir in the remaining ingredients. Spoon into potato shells. Place on tray in air-fryer basket. Cook until heated through, 5-10 minutes.

1 stuffed potato half: 316 cal., 17g fat (9g sat. fat), 42mg chol., 264mg sod., 37g carb. (3g sugars, 4g fiber), 6g pro.

CHAPTER 4

FISH, SEAFOOD & MEATLESS

When you want to shake up the usual dinner rotation, just hook the catch of the day or indulge in a fresh meatless meal. From perfectly flaky fish and seafood to kicked-up tacos, saucy pasta and even a few global-inspired dishes, these air-fryer recipes give you plenty of flavorful options.

VEGAN BUTTER CAULIFLOWER

If you follow a vegetarian diet or simply love Indian butter chicken, I encourage you to try this vegan version made with cauliflower. If you're not following a plant-based diet, you can substitute cubed chicken for the cauliflower with good results.

—*Mihaela Metaxa-Albu, London, NY*

PREP: 25 MIN. • COOK: 20 MIN. • MAKES: 4 SERVINGS

1 large head cauliflower, cut into florets
2 Tbsp. coconut oil, melted
1 Tbsp. minced fresh gingerroot
2 garlic cloves, minced
1 tsp. garam masala
¼ tsp. salt
¼ tsp. pepper

SAUCE
1 Tbsp. olive oil
½ cup chopped onion
1 Tbsp. minced fresh gingerroot
2 garlic cloves, minced
2 tsp. garam masala
2 tsp. curry powder
1 tsp. cayenne pepper, optional
1 can (15 oz.) crushed tomatoes
1 can (13.66 oz.) coconut milk
¼ tsp. salt
¼ tsp. pepper
¼ cup chopped fresh cilantro
Optional: Hot cooked rice, naan flatbreads and lime wedges

1. Preheat air fryer to 400°. In a large bowl, combine first 7 ingredients; toss to coat. In batches if necessary, place cauliflower in a single layer on greased tray in air-fryer basket. Cook until brown and crisp-tender, 8-10 minutes, turning once.

2. Meanwhile, in a large skillet, heat olive oil over medium-high heat. Add onion; cook and stir until tender, 4-5 minutes. Add ginger, garlic, garam masala, curry powder and, if desired, cayenne pepper; cook 1 minute longer. Stir in the tomatoes, coconut milk, salt and pepper. Bring to a boil; reduce heat. Simmer, uncovered, until thickened, 10-12 minutes, stirring occasionally.

3. Stir in cauliflower; sprinkle with cilantro. If desired, serve with rice, naan and lime wedges.

1½ cups: 349 cal., 27g fat (23g sat. fat), 0 chol., 584mg sod., 24g carb. (11g sugars, 7g fiber), 8g pro.

WHY YOU'LL LOVE IT...
"We ate this with naan and it was amazing! Our family loves roasted cauliflower but I've never used it as the starring element in Indian food. The sauce is creamy and aromatic from the ginger and garam masala. It was a hit with all three of my kids."
—CURLYLIS85, TASTEOFHOME.COM

BLACK BEAN CHIMICHANGAS

These chimichangas get a little love from the air fryer, so they're much healthier than their deep-fried counterparts. Black beans provide protein, and the recipe is a smart way to use up leftover rice.
—*Kimberly Hammond, Kingwood, TX*

PREP: 20 MIN. • COOK: 5 MIN./BATCH • MAKES: 6 SERVINGS

2 cans (15 oz. each) black beans, rinsed and drained
1 pkg. (8.8 oz.) ready-to-serve brown rice
⅔ cup frozen corn
⅔ cup minced fresh cilantro
⅔ cup chopped green onions
½ tsp. salt
6 whole wheat tortillas (8 in.), warmed if necessary
4 tsp. olive oil
   Optional: Guacamole and salsa

1. Preheat air fryer to 400°. In a large microwave-safe bowl, mix beans, rice and corn; microwave, covered, until heated through, 4-5 minutes, stirring halfway. Stir in the cilantro, green onions and salt.

2. To assemble, spoon ¾ cup bean mixture across the center of each tortilla. Fold bottom and sides of tortilla over filling and roll up. Brush with olive oil.

3. In batches, place seam side down on greased tray in air-fryer basket. Cook until golden brown and crispy, 2-3 minutes. If desired, serve with guacamole and salsa.

1 chimichanga: 337 cal., 5g fat (0 sat. fat), 0 chol., 602mg sod., 58g carb. (2g sugars, 10g fiber), 13g pro.

SALMON PATTIES

My mom would often fix these salmon patties when we were working late on the family farm. Feel free to add some chopped green or red peppers to the mixture.
—*Bonnie Evans, Cameron, NC*

TAKES: 25 MIN. • MAKES: 3 SERVINGS

⅓ cup finely chopped onion
1 large egg, beaten
5 saltines, crushed
½ tsp. Worcestershire sauce
¼ tsp. salt
⅛ tsp. pepper
1 can (14¾ oz.) salmon, drained, bones and skin removed
Cooking spray

1. Preheat air fryer to 375°. In a large bowl, combine the first 6 ingredients. Crumble the salmon over mixture and mix well. Shape into 6 patties.

2. Arrange patties on greased tray in air-fryer basket; spritz with cooking spray. Cook until set and golden brown, 6-8 minutes.

2 patties: 285 cal., 12g fat (3g sat. fat), 172mg chol., 876mg sod., 6g carb. (1g sugars, 0 fiber), 36g pro.

AIR-FRYING TIP

Salmon patties are done when they look golden in color, are crispy on the outside and hold their shape.

BACON-WRAPPED SCALLOPS WITH PINEAPPLE QUINOA

Bacon-wrapped scallops seem so decadent and fancy that oftentimes I forget how easy they are to prepare. Paired with a pineapple quinoa, this elegant dinner can be ready in under 30 minutes.
—Laura Greenberg, Lake Balboa, CA

TAKES: 30 MIN. • MAKES: 4 SERVINGS

1 can (14½ oz.) vegetable broth
1 cup quinoa, rinsed
¼ tsp. salt
⅛ tsp. plus ¼ tsp. pepper, divided
10 bacon strips
16 sea scallops (about 2 lbs.), side muscles removed
1 cup drained canned pineapple tidbits

1. In a small saucepan, bring broth to a boil. Add quinoa, salt and ⅛ tsp. pepper. Reduce heat; simmer, covered, 12-15 minutes or until liquid is absorbed.

2. Meanwhile, preheat air fryer to 400°. Arrange 8 strips of bacon in a single layer on tray in air-fryer basket. Cook for 3 minutes or until partially cooked but not crisp. Remove and set aside. Add the remaining 2 bacon strips; cook until crisp, 5-6 minutes. Finely chop crisp bacon strips. Cut remaining partially-cooked bacon strips lengthwise in half.

3. Wrap a halved bacon strip around each scallop; secure with a toothpick. Sprinkle with remaining pepper.

4. Arrange the scallops in a single layer on greased tray in air-fryer basket. Cook until the scallops are firm and opaque, 8-10 minutes. Discard toothpicks.

5. Remove quinoa from heat; fluff with a fork. Stir in pineapple and chopped bacon. Serve with scallops.

4 scallops with ¾ cup quinoa: 455 cal., 12g fat (3g sat. fat), 75mg chol., 1717mg sod., 45g carb. (10g sugars, 3g fiber), 41g pro.

VEGGIE BURGERS

I challenged myself to create a veggie burger that is delicious, doesn't fall apart when cooked and is easy to make. I assemble these patties ahead of time and toss them in my air fryer when I get home.
—*Sarah Tramonte, Milwaukee, WI*

PREP: 30 MIN. • COOK: 10 MIN. • MAKES: 4 SERVINGS

1 cup canned black beans, rinsed and drained
1 cup chopped walnuts
1½ tsp. ground cumin
½ tsp. ground fennel seed
¼ tsp. smoked paprika
1 Tbsp. oil from sun-dried tomatoes
¼ cup shredded carrot
1 large shallot, minced
2 Tbsp. oil-packed sun-dried tomatoes, chopped
1 garlic clove, minced
¼ cup old-fashioned oats
1 Tbsp. chia seeds
2 tsp. reduced-sodium soy sauce
½ tsp. garlic salt
Cooking spray
Optional: Barbecue sauce, toasted hamburger buns, sriracha mayo, lettuce, red onion and tomato

1. Preheat air fryer to 325°. Spread beans evenly on greased tray in air-fryer basket. Cook until beans start to split open, 3-5 minutes.

2. Meanwhile, in a large dry nonstick skillet over medium heat, cook and stir walnuts, cumin, fennel and smoked paprika until fragrant, 2-3 minutes. Remove from pan and cool. In the same skillet, heat oil from sun-dried tomatoes over medium heat. Add carrot, shallot and sun-dried tomatoes; cook and stir until tender, about 5 minutes. Add garlic; cook 1 minute longer. Remove from the heat; cool slightly.

3. Transfer carrot mixture to a food processor. Add the beans, walnut mixture, oats, chia seeds, soy sauce and garlic salt. Pulse until combined. Shape into four 4-in. patties.

4. Place patties on greased tray in air-fryer basket; spritz with cooking spray. Cook patties until browned, 6-8 minutes. If desired, baste with barbecue sauce and serve on buns with toppings of your choice.

1 burger: 337 cal., 25g fat (3g sat. fat), 0 chol., 479mg sod., 22g carb. (2g sugars, 7g fiber), 9g pro.

AIR-FRYING TIP
Save yourself some work later by assembling these mini lasagnas ahead of time. You can keep the prebaked dishes covered in your refrigerator for up to 2 days before baking them in the air fryer.

LASAGNA FOR 2

Not wanting to spend a lot of time making a full pan of lasagna on a busy evening,
I came up with this easy air-fryer recipe. I was amazed at how well it turned out.
—*Carol Mead, Los Alamos, NM*

TAKES: 25 MIN. • MAKES: 2 SERVINGS

1 cup meatless
  pasta sauce, heated
¾ cup shredded part-skim
  mozzarella cheese
½ cup 4% cottage cheese
1½ cups cooked
  wide egg noodles
2 Tbsp. grated
  Parmesan cheese
  Chopped fresh parsley,
  optional

1. Preheat air fryer to 350°. Stir together warm spaghetti sauce, mozzarella and cottage cheeses. Fold in noodles. Pour mixture into 2 greased 2-cup baking dishes that fit in air fryer. Sprinkle with Parmesan cheese.

2. Place dishes in air fryer. Cook until bubbly, about 15 minutes. If desired, top with parsley.

1 lasagna: 381 cal., 15g fat (7g sat. fat), 68mg chol., 1028mg sod., 39g carb. (14g sugars, 4g fiber), 23g pro.

TEMPEH BACON

Those following a plant-based diet shouldn't have to miss out
on the pleasures of a good BLT or a side of bacon with breakfast.
This tempeh bacon is smoky, flavorful and easy to prepare.
—*Rashanda Cobbins, Milwaukee, WI*

PREP: 5 MIN. + CHILLING • COOK: 10 MIN./BATCH • MAKES: 6 SERVINGS

3 Tbsp. liquid smoke
1 Tbsp. maple syrup
2 tsp. smoked paprika
½ tsp. ground cumin
1 pkg. (8 oz.) tempeh,
   thinly sliced

1. Whisk together liquid smoke, maple syrup, paprika and cumin in a 8-in. square baking dish; add sliced tempeh. Gently toss to coat. Cover and refrigerate at least 1 hour.

2. Preheat air fryer to 325°. In batches, place tempeh in a single layer on greased tray in air-fryer basket. Cook until golden brown, 10-12 minutes.

1 serving: 84 cal., 4g fat (1g sat. fat), 0 chol., 5mg sod., 6g carb. (2g sugars, 0 fiber), 8g pro. **Diabetic exchanges:** 1 medium-fat meat, ½ starch.

FISH TACOS

These crispy tacos are good enough to challenge the best food truck. I love that the fish is deliciously guilt-free because it's air-fried instead of deep-fried.
—*Lena Lim, Seattle, WA*

PREP: 30 MIN. • COOK: 10 MIN./BATCH • MAKES: 8 SERVINGS

¾ cup reduced-fat sour cream
1 can (4 oz.) chopped
  green chiles
1 Tbsp. fresh cilantro leaves
1 Tbsp. lime juice
4 tilapia fillets (4 oz. each)
½ cup all-purpose flour
1 large egg white, beaten
½ cup panko bread crumbs
  Cooking spray
½ tsp. salt
⅛ tsp. each white pepper,
  cayenne pepper
  and paprika
8 corn tortillas (6 in.), warmed
1 large tomato,
  finely chopped

1. Place sour cream, chiles, cilantro and lime juice in a food processor; cover and process until blended. Set aside.

2. Cut each tilapia fillet lengthwise into 2 portions. Place flour, egg white and bread crumbs in separate shallow bowls. Dip tilapia in flour, then egg white, then crumbs.

3. Preheat air fryer to 400°. In batches, arrange fillets in a single layer on greased tray in air-fryer basket; spritz with cooking spray. Cook until fish flakes easily with a fork, 10-12 minutes, turning once.

4. Combine seasonings; sprinkle over fish. Place a portion of fish on each tortilla; top with about 2 Tbsp. sour cream mixture. Sprinkle with tomato. If desired, top with additional cilantro.

1 taco: 178 cal., 3g fat (1g sat. fat), 30mg chol., 269mg sod., 22g carb. (2g sugars, 2g fiber), 16g pro. **Diabetic exchanges:** 2 lean meat, 1½ starch, ½ fat.

HOMEMADE FALAFEL

Falafel are a popular street food in the Middle East. The crispy fried chickpea fritters are crunchy on the outside, tender on the inside and full of flavor from cilantro, mint, coriander and nutty sesame seeds. They're gluten free on top of it all. Parsley can be added or used instead of mint.

—Nithya Narasimhan, Chennai, AL

PREP: 10 MIN. + CHILLING • COOK: 15 MIN./BATCH • MAKES: 16 PIECES

1 cup dried garbanzo beans
½ tsp. baking soda
1 cup fresh cilantro leaves
½ cup fresh mint leaves
5 garlic cloves
1 tsp. salt
½ tsp. pepper, optional
1 tsp. ground coriander
1 tsp. chili powder
1 tsp. sesame seeds
1 tsp. baking powder
Cooking spray

1. In a large bowl, cover beans with water. Stir in baking soda. Cover and let stand overnight. Drain beans; rinse and pat dry.

2. In a food processor, pulse cilantro and mint until finely chopped. Add beans, garlic, salt, pepper if desired, coriander and chili powder. Pulse until blended and texture of coarse meal. Transfer to a large bowl. Cover and refrigerate at least 1 hour.

3. Preheat air fryer to 375°. Stir in sesame seeds and baking powder. Shape into sixteen 2-in. balls. Arrange 8 balls in a single layer on greased tray in air-fryer basket; spritz with cooking spray. Cook until golden brown, 12-15 minutes, turning occasionally.

4 pieces: 144 cal., 4g fat (0 sat. fat), 0 chol., 762mg sod., 33g carb. (1g sugars, 16g fiber), 9g pro.

AIR-FRYING TIP

If your falafel fell apart in the air fryer, it could be because the mixture wasn't pulsed long enough in the food processor and the pieces were too large to bind together. Make sure you blend until the mixture is the texture of coarse meal.

TILAPIA FILLETS

Cooking tilapia fillets in the air fryer means dinner will be on the table in less than half an hour. It's quick and easy, and it doesn't dry out the delicate fillets.

—*Dana Alexander, Lebanon, MO*

TAKES: 20 MIN. • MAKES: 2 SERVINGS

2   tilapia fillets (6 oz. each)
1   Tbsp. butter, melted
1   tsp. Montreal
    steak seasoning
½   tsp. dried parsley flakes
¼   tsp. paprika
¼   tsp. dried thyme
⅛   tsp. onion powder
⅛   tsp. salt
⅛   tsp. pepper
    Dash garlic powder

1. Preheat air fryer to 400°. Brush fillets with butter. In a small bowl, mix remaining ingredients; sprinkle over fillets.

2. Place fillets in a single layer on greased tray in air-fryer basket. Cook until fish just begins to flake easily with a fork, 6-8 minutes.

1 fillet: 193 cal., 7g fat (4g sat. fat), 98mg chol., 594mg sod., 0 carb. (0 sugars, 0 fiber), 32g pro. **Diabetic exchanges:** 5 lean meat, 1½ fat.

BUTTERNUT SQUASH TACOS

Butternut squash tossed with southwestern spices makes a wonderful base for vegetarian tacos. I'm always looking for easy and healthy dinners for my family, and this dish is delicious!
—*Elisabeth Larsen, Pleasant Grove, UT*

PREP: 10 MIN. • COOK: 15 MIN./BATCH • MAKES: 6 SERVINGS

2 Tbsp. canola oil
1 Tbsp. chili powder
½ tsp. ground cumin
½ tsp. ground coriander
½ tsp. salt
¼ tsp. cayenne pepper
1 medium butternut squash (3 to 4 lbs.), peeled and cut into ½-in. pieces
12 corn tortillas (6 in.), warmed
1 cup crumbled queso fresco or feta cheese
1 medium ripe avocado, peeled and sliced thin
¼ cup diced red onion
Pico de gallo, optional

1. Preheat air fryer to 400°. Combine the first 6 ingredients. Add squash pieces; toss to coat. In batches, arrange squash in a single layer on greased tray in air-fryer basket. Cook until tender, 15-20 minutes.

2. Divide squash evenly among tortillas. Top with queso fresco, avocado and red onion. If desired, serve with pico de gallo.

2 tacos: 353 cal., 13g fat (3g sat. fat), 13mg chol., 322mg sod., 54g carb. (7g sugars, 13g fiber), 11g pro.

WHY YOU'LL LOVE IT...
"Excellent. Very flavorful. We added a can of drained and rinsed black beans (seasoned with garlic powder, salt and cumin) to the tacos for extra protein (copied from one of our favorite restaurants). These are also amazing topped with some sour cream. Will make again and again."
—BRANDHORSTB, TASTEOFHOME.COM

CHAPTER 5

PORK ENTREES

Have dinner on the lable in a flash thanks to these quick and easy air-fried pork recipes. With succulent chops drizzled with rhubarb sauce, classic sausage pizza or a traditional sugar-glazed ham, you can't go wrong!

HAM STEAK WITH PINEAPPLE SALSA

Ham and pineapple are such a wonderful combination. I love to add this pineapple salsa to air-fried ham steaks for a quick and easy dinner everyone loves.
—Dawn Wilson, Buena Vista, CO

TAKES: 25 MIN. • MAKES: 4 SERVINGS

1 can (8 oz.) crushed pineapple, drained
2 Tbsp. orange marmalade
1 Tbsp. minced fresh cilantro
2 tsp. finely chopped seeded jalapeno pepper
2 tsp. lime juice
¼ tsp. salt
1 bone-in fully cooked ham steak (1½ lbs.)

1. Preheat air fryer to 400°. In a small bowl, mix the first 6 ingredients. Refrigerate until serving.

2. Place ham steak on greased tray in air-fryer basket. Cook until a thermometer reads 140°, 4-6 minutes. Cut ham into serving-size pieces. Serve with pineapple salsa.

Note: Wear disposable gloves when cutting hot peppers; the oils can burn skin. Avoid touching your face.

1 serving: 228 cal., 8g fat (3g sat. fat), 65mg chol., 1366mg sod., 20g carb. (17g sugars, 1g fiber), 21g pro.

WHY YOU'LL LOVE IT...
"This is just the right amount of kick that ham steaks need, with the great taste of fruit. Only had tidbits, but it was wonderful!"
—PLUMJAS30, TASTEOFHOME.COM

AIR-FRYING TIP

The tenderloin is the full length of the pork's loin. It can be cooked whole or sliced crosswise into medallions. Tender and mild in flavor, this type of pork is best when rubbed with spices, marinated or sauced.

PORK TENDERLOIN

I originally developed this air-fryer pork tenderloin recipe to cook on the stove and finish in the oven, but you can make it even quicker in an air fryer—and it's just as tasty.

—*Lynn Faria, Southington, CT*

PREP: 10 MIN. • COOK: 20 MIN. + STANDING • MAKES: 2 SERVINGS

1 pork tenderloin (¾ lb.)
1 Tbsp. spicy brown mustard
2 tsp. canola oil
1 tsp. garlic powder
1 tsp. onion powder
½ tsp. pepper

Preheat air fryer to 375°. Trim silver skin from tenderloin if desired; pat dry. In a small bowl, stir together remaining ingredients; spread over tenderloin. Place on a greased tray in the air-fryer basket. Cook until a thermometer reads 145°, 18-20 minutes. Let stand 10 minutes before slicing.

5 oz. cooked pork: 257 cal., 11g fat (2g sat. fat), 95mg chol., 145mg sod., 2g carb. (0 sugars, 0 fiber), 34g pro. **Diabetic exchanges:** 5 lean meat, 1 fat.

THAI PORK SATAY

I like to keep meals simple but interesting and delicious. This pork satay
does just that. Marinate it overnight and then when you're ready
for dinner, just pop the skewers in the air fryer.
—*Stephanie Butz, Portland, OR*

PREP: 30 MIN. + MARINATING • COOK: 10 MIN./BATCH • MAKES: 6 SERVINGS

1 cup coconut milk
3 garlic cloves, minced
2 Tbsp. ground cumin
1 Tbsp. ground coriander
1 Tbsp. brown sugar
1 Tbsp. canola oil
1½ tsp. salt
1 tsp. paprika
1 tsp. curry powder
 Dash crushed
 red pepper flakes
1½ lbs. boneless pork,
 cut into ½-in. cubes

PEANUT DIPPING SAUCE
1 cup water
⅔ cup creamy peanut butter
1 garlic clove, minced
2 Tbsp. brown sugar
2 Tbsp. soy sauce
2 tsp. lemon juice
 Dash crushed
 red pepper flakes
 Hot cooked jasmine rice,
 optional

1. In a bowl or shallow dish, combine the first 10 ingredients; add pork and turn to coat. Cover and refrigerate overnight. Drain pork, discarding marinade.

2. For sauce, in a small saucepan, combine water, peanut butter and garlic. Cook and stir over medium heat until thickened, about 2 minutes. Whisk in brown sugar, soy sauce, lemon juice and pepper flakes until blended; keep warm.

3. Preheat air fryer to 375°. Thread pork onto 12 metal or soaked wooden skewers that fit in air fryer. In batches, place skewers on greased tray in air-fryer basket. Cook until the pork is no longer pink, 6-8 minutes per batch, turning occasionally.

4. Serve skewers with peanut sauce and, if desired, rice.

2 skewers: 454 cal., 30g fat (12g sat. fat), 67mg chol., 1082mg sod., 16g carb. (10g sugars, 3g fiber), 32g pro.

HAM & LEEK PIES

After I cook a big ham, I'm always finding new ways to use up the leftovers.
I love these little pot pies. I can whip them up at a moment's notice
and pop them into the air fryer for a quick dinner.
—*Bonny Tillman, Acworth, GA*

PREP: 40 MIN. • COOK: 15 MIN. • MAKES: 4 SERVINGS

¼ cup butter, cubed
4 cups sliced leeks
(white portion only)
½ lb. sliced fresh mushrooms
3 medium carrots, sliced
½ cup all-purpose flour
1¼ cups 2% milk
1¼ cups vegetable broth
1¾ cups cubed fully
cooked ham
2 Tbsp. minced fresh parsley
¼ to ½ tsp. ground nutmeg
Dash pepper
1 sheet frozen puff
pastry, thawed
1 large egg, lightly beaten

1. In a large saucepan, heat butter over medium-high heat. Add leeks, mushrooms and carrots; cook and stir until tender.

2. Stir in flour until blended. Gradually stir in milk and broth. Bring to a boil over medium heat, stirring constantly; cook and stir until thickened, about 2 minutes. Remove from heat; stir in ham, parsley, nutmeg and pepper.

3. Preheat air fryer to 400°. On a lightly floured surface, unfold puff pastry; roll out to ¼-in. thickness. Using a 10-oz. ramekin as a template, cut out 4 tops for pies. Fill 4 greased 10-oz. ramekins with hot leek mixture; top with pastry. Cut slits in pastry. Brush tops with egg.

4. In batches if necessary, place ramekins in air fryer. Cook until golden brown, 12-15 minutes. Let pies stand 5 minutes before serving.

1 pie: 682 cal., 34g fat (13g sat. fat), 119mg chol., 1349mg sod., 70g carb. (11g sugars, 8g fiber), 27g pro.

BONE-IN PORK CHOPS WITH RHUBARB

When rhubarb starts popping up in gardens and farmers' markets,
I get ready to prepare this quick and simple pork chop dish.
—*Bonnie Bufford, Nicholson, PA*

TAKES: 20 MIN. • MAKES: 2 SERVINGS

2   bone-in pork loin chops
    (½ to ¾ in. thick)
¼   tsp. salt
¼   tsp. pepper
2   Tbsp. butter
½   lb. fresh or frozen
    rhubarb, chopped
1   Tbsp. honey
⅛   tsp. ground cinnamon
1½ tsp. minced fresh parsley

1. Preheat air fryer to 400°. Sprinkle pork chops with salt and pepper. Place chopson greased tray in air-fryer basket. Cook until a thermometer reads 145°, 4-5 minutes on each side.

2. Meanwhile, in a saucepan, melt butter over medium heat. Add rhubarb, honey and cinnamon; cook until rhubarb is tender, about 5 minutes. Serve sauce over pork chops. Sprinkle with parsley.

1 pork chop: 478 cal., 30g fat (14g sat. fat), 142mg chol., 468mg sod., 14g carb. (10g sugars, 2g fiber), 37g pro.

WHY YOU'LL LOVE IT...
"Easy, quick, with a browned exterior and tender inside. Love the savory and sweet combo of flavors, although a little more honey would make the dish even better."
—FROMBRAZILTOYOU.ORG, TASTEOFHOME.COM

AIR-FRYING TIP
This pork loin will last 3 to 4 days in an airtight container in the refrigerator.

PORK LOIN ROAST

After lots of tweaking, I've come up with the perfect pork loin recipe.
It's simple to pull together, and the leftovers are fantastic.
—*DeEtta Rasmussen, Fort Madison, IA*

PREP: 15 MIN. • COOK: 50 MIN. + STANDING • MAKES: 8 SERVINGS

¼ cup reduced-sodium
    soy sauce
6 garlic cloves, minced
1 Tbsp. each minced fresh
    basil, rosemary and sage
1 Tbsp. ground mustard
1 pork loin roast (3½ lbs.)
8 green onions, chopped
2 Tbsp. butter
¼ cup brown gravy mix
2½ cups beef broth
1¼ cups sour cream
2 Tbsp. prepared horseradish

1. Preheat air fryer to 325°. In a small bowl, combine soy sauce, garlic, herbs and mustard; rub over roast. Place on greased tray in air-fryer basket. Cook until a thermometer inserted in pork reads 145°, 50-70 minutes. Remove roast from air fryer; tent with foil. Let stand 15 minutes before slicing.

2. Meanwhile, in a large saucepan, saute onions in butter until tender. Combine gravy mix and broth until smooth; stir into pan. Bring to a boil. Reduce heat; cook and stir until thickened. Stir in sour cream and horseradish; heat through (do not boil). Serve with pork.

6 oz. cooked pork with ¼ cup gravy: 388 cal., 20g fat (10g sat. fat), 133mg chol., 906mg sod., 7g carb. (3g sugars, 1g fiber), 42g pro.

SAUSAGE PIZZAS

I've always loved personal-sized pizzas, and when I figured out
how to make them in my air fryer, I was in pizza heaven! It's so easy, and
now that my boys can customize their own, everyone is happy.
—*Margo Zoerner, Pleasant Prairie, WI*

PREP: 30 MIN. • BAKE: 10 MIN./BATCH • MAKES: 4 PIZZAS

1   loaf (1 lb.) frozen
    bread dough, thawed
1   cup pizza sauce
½   lb. bulk Italian sausage,
    cooked and drained
1⅓ cups shredded part-skim
    mozzarella cheese
1   small green pepper,
    sliced into rings
1   tsp. dried oregano
    Crushed red pepper flakes,
    optional

1. On a lightly floured surface, roll and stretch dough into four
4-in. circles. Cover; let rest for 10 minutes.

2. Preheat air fryer to 400°. Roll and stretch each dough into
a 6-in. circle. Place 1 crust on greased tray in air-fryer basket.
Carefully spread with ¼ cup pizza sauce, ⅓ cup sausage,
⅓ cup cheese, a fourth of green pepper rings and a pinch
of oregano. Cook until crust is golden brown, 6-8 minutes.
If desired, sprinkle with red pepper flakes. Repeat with
remaining ingredients.

1 pizza: 615 cal., 26g fat (9g sat. fat), 58mg chol., 1513mg sod., 64g carb. (9g sugars,
6g fiber), 29g pro.

THIN PORK CHOPS

Instant mashed potatoes and bread crumbs have a similar texture so I wondered how they would be as a breading for pork chops. I was pleased with the results! Now this is the only way I make pork chops.
—*Carrie Farias, Oak Ridge, NJ*

PREP: 15 MIN. • COOK: 5 MIN./BATCH • MAKES: 4 SERVINGS

1 large egg
2 Tbsp. fat-free milk
2 Tbsp. Dijon mustard
¾ cup panko bread crumbs
¾ cup mashed potato flakes
2 tsp. ground mustard
2 tsp. minced fresh sage
⅓ cup all-purpose flour
8 thin boneless pork loin chops (2 oz. each)
½ tsp. salt
Cooking spray

1. In a shallow bowl, whisk the egg, milk and Dijon mustard. In another shallow bowl, mix bread crumbs, potato flakes, ground mustard and sage. Place flour in another shallow bowl. Sprinkle pork with salt.

2. Preheat air fryer to 400°. Dip pork in flour to coat both sides; shake off excess. Dip in egg mixture, then in the bread crumb mixture, patting to help coating adhere.

3. In batches, place chops on greased tray in air-fryer basket; spritz with the cooking spray. Cook until a thermometer reads at least 145°, 5-6 minutes, turning once.

2 pork chops: 297 cal., 9g fat (3g sat. fat), 101mg chol., 565mg sod., 22g carb. (1g sugars, 1g fiber), 27g pro. **Diabetic exchanges:** 3 lean meat, 1½ starch, 1 fat.

BROWN SUGAR HAM

This simple old-fashioned glaze tastes just like the kind Grandma used to make. The mustard and vinegar counter the sweetness from the brown sugar and add a pleasant tangy flavor.

—Carol Strong Battle, Heathsville, VA

PREP: 5 MIN. • COOK: 1¼ HOURS • MAKES: 14 SERVINGS

1 fully cooked bone-in ham (5 to 7 lbs.)
1 cup packed brown sugar
2 tsp. prepared mustard
1 to 2 Tbsp. cider vinegar

AIR-FRYING TIP
It's not just *how* you glaze a ham, but also *when* you glaze. Apply the glaze liberally over the entire ham 15 to 20 minutes before it's finished cooking. If you glaze it prior to cooking, the coating will likely burn.

1. Preheat air fryer to 300°. Place ham on a double-thickness of heavy-duty aluminum foil. Using a sharp knife, score surface of ham with ¼-in.-deep cuts in a diamond pattern; seal foil. Place in air fryer. Cook until a thermometer reads 130°, 1-1½ hours.

2. Meanwhile, in a small bowl, combine brown sugar, mustard and enough vinegar to make a thick paste. Remove ham from air fryer. Spread sugar mixture over ham. Cook, uncovered, until a thermometer reads 140°, 15-20 minutes longer, tenting with foil if glaze starts to brown.

4 oz. ham: 196 cal., 4g fat (1g sat. fat), 71mg chol., 863mg sod., 16g carb. (16g sugars, 0 fiber), 24g pro.

CHAPTER 6

POULTRY ENTREES

Economical and versatile, chicken and turkey are popular
standbys for hearty weeknight dinners. From juicy wings
and zesty fajitas to comforting potpies and other classics,
these cravable air-fried dishes will have you swooning
over their golden color and crispy crunch.

CHICKEN PICCATA POCKETS

My husband loves Chicken Piccata. I tried making it in a puff pastry pocket with a bit of cream cheese, and it tasted sensational. When he took leftovers to work, everyone asked what smelled so amazing.
—*Arlene Erlbach, Morton Grove, IL*

PREP: 15 MIN. • COOK: 20 MIN. • MAKES: 4 SERVINGS

1 pkg. (8 oz.) cream cheese, softened
2 Tbsp. lemon juice
¼ tsp. salt
¼ tsp. pepper
2 Tbsp. capers, drained
1 large shallot, finely chopped
1 sheet frozen puff pastry, thawed
4 chicken tenderloins, cubed
1 large egg, well beaten
1 Tbsp. water
4 thin lemon slices
2 Tbsp. chopped fresh parsley

1. Preheat air fryer to 400°. In a bowl, beat cream cheese, lemon juice, salt and pepper on medium speed until well combined. Fold in capers and shallot.

2. Unfold puff pastry; roll into a 12-in. square. Cut into 4 smaller squares. Spread cream cheese mixture over squares to within ¼ in. of edges; top with chicken.

3. Fold a corner of each pastry square over chicken, forming a triangle. Pinch triangle edges to seal and flatten with fork for tighter seal. Whisk egg and water; brush over pastry pockets, including edges. Discard leftover egg mixture. Pierce each pocket twice with a fork to vent.

4. Place in a single layer on greased tray in air-fryer basket. Cook until golden brown, 18-25 minutes. Remove from air fryer; cool 5 minutes. Serve pockets with lemon slices and parsley.

Freeze option: Cover and freeze unbaked pockets on a waxed paper-lined baking sheet until firm. Transfer to an airtight container; return to freezer. To use, cook as directed, increasing time by about 5 minutes.

1 chicken pocket: 564 cal., 38g fat (16g sat. fat), 120mg chol., 669mg sod., 41g carb. (3g sugars, 5g fiber), 18g pro.

CHICKEN YAKITORI

This dish is a take on the street food I grew up with in Tokyo.
Traditionally it's grilled, but the air fryer makes quick and easy work
of it without having to fire up the grill. I serve it with rice.
—*Lindsay Howerton-Hastings, Greenville, SC*

PREP: 15 MIN. • COOK: 30 MIN. • MAKES: 6 SERVINGS

½ cup mirin (sweet rice wine)
½ cup sake
½ cup soy sauce
1 Tbsp. sugar
2 large sweet red peppers, cut into 2-in. pieces
2 lbs. boneless skinless chicken thighs
1 bunch green onions

1. In a small saucepan, combine the first 4 ingredients. Bring to a boil over medium-high heat. Remove from heat; set aside half the mixture for serving.

2. Preheat air fryer to 350°. Thread peppers onto 2 metal or soaked wooden skewers that fit into air fryer. Thread chicken onto 6 metal or soaked wooden skewers that fit into air fryer. In batches, place chicken skewers in a single layer on greased tray in air-fryer basket. Cook until chicken is no longer pink, 10-12 minutes, turning occasionally and basting frequently with soy sauce mixture during the last 3 minutes. Remove and keep warm.

3. Place pepper skewers in a single layer on greased tray in air-fryer basket. Cook until the vegetables are crisp-tender, 4-5 minutes, turning occasionally. Remove and set aside. Add the onions in a single layer on greased tray in air-fryer basket. Cook until tender and slightly charred, 3-4 minutes, turning occasionally. Serve chicken and vegetables with reserved sauce for dipping.

1 serving: 332 cal., 11g fat (3g sat. fat), 101mg chol., 1316mg sod., 14g carb. (11g sugars, 1g fiber), 32g pro.

CHICKEN PARMESAN

Quick, simple and oh-so-tasty, this air-fried Chicken Parmesan is the perfect weeknight dish to have on hand. It's just as crispy as the classic, if not crispier!
—Taste of Home *Test Kitchen*

TAKES: 20 MIN. • MAKES: 4 SERVINGS

2 large eggs
½ cup seasoned bread crumbs
⅓ cup grated Parmesan cheese
¼ tsp. pepper
4 boneless skinless chicken breast halves (6 oz. each)
1 cup pasta sauce
1 cup shredded mozzarella cheese
Optional: Chopped fresh basil and hot cooked pasta

1. Preheat air fryer to 375°. In a shallow bowl, lightly beat eggs. In another shallow bowl, combine bread crumbs, Parmesan and pepper. Dip chicken in egg, then coat with crumb mixture.

2. Place chicken in a single layer on greased tray in air-fryer basket. Cook until a thermometer reads 165°, 10-12 minutes, turning halfway through. Top chicken with sauce and cheese. Cook until cheese is melted, 3-4 minutes. If desired, sprinkle with chopped basil and additional Parmesan cheese and serve with pasta.

1 chicken breast half: 416 cal., 16g fat (7g sat. fat), 215mg chol., 863mg sod., 18g carb. (6g sugars, 2g fiber), 49g pro.

WHY YOU'LL LOVE IT...
"Simple and delicious! I made with panko crumbs and added Italian seasoning. Served with angel hair pasta and homemade sauce. This recipe is a keeper!"
—KIM6822, TASTEOFHOME.COM

TURKEY WINGS

My family loves air-fried chicken wings, so I thought, why not go big and try the recipe with turkey wings? These are a hit every time I serve them.
—*Francis Mitchell, Brooklyn, NY*

PREP: 15 MIN. + MARINATING • COOK: 25 MIN. • MAKES: 6 SERVINGS

3 lbs. turkey wings
1¼ cups barbecue sauce
2 green onions, sliced
1 tsp. paprika
½ tsp. garlic powder
½ tsp. salt
½ tsp. pepper
¼ tsp. soy sauce

1. Cut turkey wings into sections; discard wing tips. In a large shallow dish, combine remaining ingredients; add wing sections. Turn to coat; refrigerate, covered, 6-8 hours or overnight.

2. Preheat air fryer to 350°. Drain wings, discarding marinade. Place wings in a single layer on greased tray in air-fryer basket. Cook until a thermometer reads 170° and turkey is tender, roughly 25-30 minutes.

1 turkey wing: 280 cal., 14g fat (4g sat. fat), 88mg chol., 307mg sod., 7g carb. (6g sugars, 0 fiber), 30g pro.

ROTISSERIE CHICKEN

Get ready for the most tender, juicy chicken you've ever had in your life.
This air-fried version rivals even the best store-bought rotisserie chicken.
—*Dawn Parker, Surrey, BC*

PREP: 5 MIN. • COOK: 65 MIN. + STANDING • MAKES: 6 SERVINGS

1 broiler/fryer chicken
(3 to 4 lbs.)
1 Tbsp. olive oil
1 Tbsp. seasoned salt

AIR-FRYING TIP
At the *Taste of Home* Test Kitchen, we like to use air fryers with a 5-quart capacity or larger. If you find your chicken is too big or your air fryer too small you can always cut the chicken into pieces and adjust your cooking time.

Preheat air fryer to 350°. Brush outside of chicken with olive oil and sprinkle with seasoned salt. Place the chicken, breast side down, on tray in air-fryer basket; cook 30 minutes. Flip chicken and cook until a thermometer inserted in thickest part of thigh reads 170°-175°, 35-40 minutes longer. Remove chicken; let stand 15 minutes before carving.

5 oz. cooked chicken: 313 cal., 19g fat (5g sat. fat), 104mg chol., 850mg sod., 0 carb. (0 sugars, 0 fiber), 33g pro.

ASPARAGUS-STUFFED CHICKEN ROLLS

This dish looks elegant, but is quite simple to make. I frequently serve it to company but also make it on weeknights, especially when asparagus is in season.
—Louise Ambrose, Kingston, NY

PREP: 20 MIN. • COOK: 15 MIN. • MAKES: 2 SERVINGS

- 8 fresh asparagus spears
- 2 boneless skinless chicken breast halves (5 oz. each)
- 1 Tbsp. Dijon mustard
- 4 fresh sage leaves
- 2 slices provolone cheese (1 oz. each)
- 2 slices deli ham (¾ oz. each)
- ¼ cup all-purpose flour
- 1 large egg, lightly beaten
- ½ cup dry bread crumbs
- ¼ cup grated Parmesan cheese
  Cooking spray

1. In a large skillet, bring ½ in. of water to a boil. Add asparagus; cover and boil for 3 minutes. Drain and immediately place the asparagus in ice water. Drain and pat dry.

2. Flatten chicken to ¼-in. thickness. Spread mustard over 1 side of each chicken breast. Down the center of each, place 2 sage leaves, a cheese slice, ham slice and 4 asparagus spears. Fold chicken over asparagus; secure with toothpicks.

3. Preheat air fryer to 325°. Place the flour and egg in separate shallow bowls. In another shallow bowl, combine bread crumbs and Parmesan cheese. Dip chicken in the flour, egg, then bread crumb mixture.

4. Place chicken in a single layer on greased tray in air-fryer basket; spritz with cooking spray. Cook until chicken is no longer pink, 15-20 minutes. Discard toothpicks.

1 stuffed chicken breast half: 382 cal., 15g fat (7g sat. fat), 167mg chol., 849mg sod., 14g carb. (2g sugars, 1g fiber), 46g pro.

CRISPY ORANGE CHICKEN

I love the orange chicken from my local Chinese restaurant, but I think this tangy homemade version is pretty close to the original...and it's so easy.
—*Darlene Brenden, Salem, OR*

TAKES: 30 MIN. • MAKES: 4 SERVINGS

16 oz. frozen popcorn chicken (about 4 cups)
1 Tbsp. canola oil
2 medium carrots, thinly sliced
1 garlic clove, minced
1½ tsp. grated orange zest
1 cup orange juice
⅓ cup hoisin sauce
3 Tbsp. sugar
¼ tsp. salt
¼ tsp. pepper
Dash cayenne pepper
Hot cooked rice

1. Air-fry popcorn chicken according to package directions.

2. Meanwhile, in a large skillet, heat oil over medium-high heat. Add carrots; cook and stir until tender, 3-5 minutes. Add garlic; cook 1 minute longer. Stir in orange zest, juice, hoisin sauce, sugar and seasonings; bring to a boil. Reduce heat; simmer, uncovered, until thickened, 4-6 minutes, stirring constantly.

3. Add chicken to skillet; toss to coat. Serve with rice.

1 cup: 447 cal., 20g fat (3g sat. fat), 35mg chol., 1287mg sod., 55g carb. (25g sugars, 3g fiber), 14g pro.

WHY YOU'LL LOVE IT...
"So yummy! I added broccoli, chunks of onion and red bell pepper. Loved everything about this."
—LBERIKSEN, TASTEOFHOME.COM

BARBECUE CHICKEN LEGS

For years I tried to find the perfect bottled barbecue sauce. I finally mixed up my own using ketchup, honey and brown mustard. It's delicious slathered on any cut of chicken, especially drumsticks.
—*Kathleen Criddle, Lake Worth, FL*

PREP: 25 MIN. • COOK: 15 MIN. • MAKES: 8 SERVINGS

2 cups ketchup
⅔ cup honey
⅓ cup packed brown sugar
2 Tbsp. finely chopped
    sweet onion
2 Tbsp. spicy brown mustard
4 garlic cloves, minced
1 Tbsp. Worcestershire sauce
1 Tbsp. cider vinegar
16 chicken drumsticks

1. In a large saucepan, mix the first 8 ingredients; bring to a boil. Reduce heat; simmer, uncovered, 15-20 minutes to allow flavors to blend, stirring occasionally. Reserve 2 cups sauce for serving.

2. Preheat air fryer to 375°. In batches, place chicken in a single layer on greased tray in air-fryer basket. Cook until a thermometer reads 170°-175°, 15-20 minutes, turning occasionally and brushing generously with remaining sauce during the last 5 minutes. Serve with reserved sauce.

2 chicken drumsticks with ¼ cup sauce: 422 cal., 12g fat (3g sat. fat), 95mg chol., 909mg sod., 49g carb. (48g sugars, 0 fiber), 29g pro.

TEST KITCHEN TIP: If your drumsticks are frozen, you can still cook them in the air fryer. Just allow for a longer cook time and use a pen thermometer to make sure the chicken reaches an internal temperature of at least 170°.

SPICY TURKEY TENDERLOIN

Serve this kicked-up turkey tenderloin for a zesty weeknight meal or on Thanksgiving when you have a small group and want something out of the ordinary. It's easy to double if you have space in your air fryer.
—*Sharon Skildum, Maple Grove, MN*

PREP: 20 MIN. • COOK: 15 MIN. + STANDING • MAKES: 2 SERVINGS

½ tsp. chili powder
½ tsp. ground cumin
¼ to ½ tsp. salt
⅛ tsp. cayenne pepper
1 turkey breast
   tenderloin (½ lb.)
3 Tbsp. chopped onion
2 Tbsp. chopped
   jalapeno pepper
1 tsp. olive oil
1 cup canned black beans,
   rinsed and drained
½ cup frozen corn, thawed
3 Tbsp. chopped fresh tomato
4 tsp. picante sauce
1 Tbsp. minced fresh cilantro
   Lime wedges

1. Preheat air fryer to 350° for 5-10 minutes. In a small bowl, combine chili powder, cumin, salt and cayenne. Sprinkle half the spice mixture over turkey. Place turkey on greased tray in air-fryer basket. Cook until a thermometer inserted into thickest portion reads 165°, 15-20 minutes. Let turkey stand 10 minutes before slicing.

2. Meanwhile, in a small skillet, saute onion and jalapeno in oil until crisp-tender. Transfer to a bowl. Add beans, corn, tomato, picante sauce, cilantro and remaining spice mixture. Serve turkey with salsa and lime wedges.

1 serving: 290 cal., 4g fat (0 sat. fat), 45mg chol., 696mg sod., 29g carb. (4g sugars, 7g fiber), 36g pro. **Diabetic exchanges:** 4 lean meat, 2 starch, ½ fat.

AIR-FRYING TIP

Make sure to let the tenderloin rest for a few minutes before cutting it into slices. This gives the juices time to redistribute throughout the meat and will prevent them from seeping out when cutting into it.

BARBECUE CHICKEN

You don't need a long list of ingredients to make tender barbecue chicken that tastes as if it's fresh off the grill. The apple flavor is subtle but makes this air-fried version stand out from the rest.
—*Darla Andrews, Boerne, TX*

TAKES: 25 MIN. • MAKES: 4 SERVINGS

4 boneless skinless chicken breast halves (6 oz. each)
½ tsp. pepper
⅔ cup chunky applesauce
⅔ cup spicy barbecue sauce
2 Tbsp. brown sugar
1 tsp. chili powder

1. Preheat air fryer to 375°. Sprinkle chicken with pepper. Place chicken, skin-side down, on tray in air-fryer basket. Cook until golden brown, 15-18 minutes. Transfer chicken to platter; remove excess fat from air fryer to prevent smoking.

2. In a small bowl, combine remaining ingredients; brush over chicken. Return chicken to air fryer. Cook until a thermometer reads 165°, 5-7 minutes.

1 chicken breast half: 317 cal., 4g fat (1g sat. fat), 94mg chol., 570mg sod., 33g carb. (28g sugars, 1g fiber), 35g pro.

CHICKEN CUTLET

If you're looking for a quick and easy lunch or dinner, try a breaded cutlet.
The flavor of Parmesan cheese in the coating complements the chicken.
—*Marie Hoyer, Lewistown, MT*

TAKES: 20 MIN. • MAKES: 1 SERVING

1 tsp. all-purpose flour
Dash each garlic powder,
onion powder and pepper
2 Tbsp. grated
Parmesan cheese
2 Tbsp. buttermilk
3 Tbsp. seasoned
bread crumbs
1 boneless skinless chicken
breast half (6 oz.)
Cooking spray

1. In a shallow bowl, combine flour, garlic powder, onion powder and pepper. In another bowl, combine cheese and buttermilk. Place bread crumbs in a third shallow bowl.

2. Preheat air fryer to 400°. Flatten chicken to ¼-in. thickness. Coat chicken with flour mixture; dip in buttermilk, then coat with crumbs. Place chicken on greased tray in air-fryer basket; spritz with cooking spray. Cook until golden brown and no longer pink, 8-10 minutes, turning once.

1 cutlet: 333 cal., 8g fat (3g sat. fat), 104mg chol., 628mg sod., 20g carb. (3g sugars, 2g fiber), 41g pro. **Diabetic exchanges:** 5 lean meat, 1 starch, ½ fat.

CORNISH HENS

Who says Cornish hens have to be for special occasions? Their small size is perfect for one, and they cook quickly and stay juicy.
—Taste of Home *Test Kitchen*

PREP: 20 MIN. • COOK: 45 MIN. • MAKES: 2 SERVINGS

2 Cornish game hens
  (20 to 24 oz. each)
12 fresh sage leaves
4 lemon wedges
6 green onions, cut into
  2-in. lengths, divided
2 Tbsp. butter, melted
1 Tbsp. olive oil
1 Tbsp. lemon juice
2 garlic cloves, minced
1 tsp. kosher salt or sea salt
¼ tsp. coarsely ground pepper
6 small red potatoes, halved

1. Preheat air fryer to 350°. Gently lift skin from hen breasts and place sage leaves under skin. Place lemon wedges and a third of the onions in the cavities. Tuck wings under hens; tie the legs together. Arrange hens on greased tray in air-fryer basket. In a small bowl, combine butter, oil, lemon juice and garlic; brush half of the mixture over hens. Sprinkle with salt and pepper.

2. Add potatoes and remaining onions to air fryer. Cook until a thermometer inserted in thickest part of thigh reads 170°-175° and potatoes are tender, 45-50 minutes, brushing hens with remaining butter mixture halfway through.

1 serving: 984 cal., 68g fat (22g sat. fat), 381mg chol., 1239mg sod., 29g carb. (3g sugars, 4g fiber), 64g pro.

TEST KITCHEN TIP: A Cornish hen looks like a miniature chicken. The birds' small size and young age lend a delicious flavor and juicy, tender flesh when cooked. Because they're so small, these little game hens cook more quickly than a standard-size chicken, making them ideal for roasting in an air fryer.

MEDITERRANEAN TURKEY POTPIES

Your family and friends will love these comforting potpies that boast a little Mediterranean flair. If you don't have turkey, cooked chicken works just as well.
—*Marie Rizzio, Interlochen, MI*

PREP: 30 MIN. • COOK: 15 MIN. • MAKES: 6 SERVINGS

- 2 medium onions, thinly sliced
- 2 tsp. olive oil
- 3 garlic cloves, minced
- 3 Tbsp. all-purpose flour
- 1¼ cups reduced-sodium chicken broth
- 1 can (14½ oz.) no-salt-added diced tomatoes, undrained
- 2½ cups cubed cooked turkey breast
- 1 can (14 oz.) water-packed artichoke hearts, rinsed, drained and sliced
- ½ cup pitted ripe olives, halved
- ¼ cup sliced pepperoncini
- 1 Tbsp. minced fresh oregano or 1 tsp. dried oregano
- ¼ tsp. pepper

CRUST
- 1 loaf (1 lb.) frozen pizza dough, thawed
- 1 large egg white
- 1 tsp. minced fresh oregano or ¼ tsp. dried oregano

1. In a Dutch oven, saute onions in oil until tender. Add garlic; cook 2 minutes longer. In a small bowl, whisk flour and broth until smooth; gradually stir into onion mixture. Stir in tomatoes. Bring to a boil; cook and stir for 2 minutes or until thickened.

2. Remove from the heat. Add the turkey, artichokes, olives, pepperoncini, oregano and pepper; stir gently. Divide turkey mixture among six 10-oz. ramekins.

3. Preheat air fryer to 375°. Roll out 2 oz. of pizza dough to fit each ramekin (reserve remaining dough for another use). Cut slits in dough; place over filling. Press to seal edges. Combine egg white and oregano; brush over dough.

4. Place ramekins on tray in air-fryer basket. Cook until crusts are golden brown, 15-20 minutes.

1 potpie: 323 cal., 6g fat (1g sat. fat), 47mg chol., 578mg sod., 39g carb. (4g sugars, 3g fiber), 26g pro. **Diabetic exchanges:** 2 starch, 2 vegetable, 2 lean meat, ½ fat.

AIR-FRYING TIP
Following this recipe ensures you'll have fully cooked chicken, but it doesn't hurt to double-check the internal temperature. If your chicken reads an internal temperature of 165°F, you're good to go.

CHICKEN FAJITAS

If the only time you indulge in fajitas is at Mexican restaurants,
you're missing out on some of the best—made right at home in the air fryer!
These are simple to put together and don't leave a mess afterward.
—*Ashley Lecker, Green Bay, WI*

PREP: 20 MIN. + MARINATING • COOK: 10 MIN./BATCH • MAKES: 8 SERVINGS

2 Tbsp. canola oil
3 Tbsp. lime juice, divided
1½ tsp. grated lime zest
1 tsp. chili powder
¾ tsp. garlic powder, divided
½ tsp. onion powder
½ tsp. ground cumin
¼ tsp. cayenne pepper
¼ tsp. pepper
2 lbs. boneless skinless chicken breasts, cut into thin strips
½ tsp. salt
1 large sweet red pepper and large green pepper, thinly sliced
1 medium onion, thinly sliced
16 corn tortillas (6 in.)
   Lime wedges
   Optional: Sour cream and chopped cilantro

1. In a bowl or shallow dish, combine oil, 2 Tbsp. lime juice, lime zest, chili powder, ½ tsp. garlic powder, onion powder, cumin, cayenne pepper and pepper. Add chicken and turn to coat. Refrigerate at least 2 hours.

2. Preheat air fryer to 400°. Drain chicken, discarding marinade. Season chicken with salt. In batches, arrange the chicken in a single layer on greased tray in air-fryer basket; cook, stirring occasionally, until no longer pink, 6-8 minutes. Remove chicken; set aside.

3. In a large bowl, toss the peppers, onion, remaining 1 Tbsp. lime juice and remaining ¼ tsp. garlic powder; add ingredients to air fryer. Cook, stirring occasionally, until tender, 4-5 minutes. Return chicken to air fryer; heat through. Serve with tortillas and lime wedges. If desired, top with sour cream and cilantro.

2 fajitas: 270 cal., 8g fat (1g sat. fat), 63mg chol., 236mg sod., 26g carb. (2g sugars, 4g fiber), 26g pro. **Diabetic exchanges:** 3 lean meat, 2 starch.

CORNFLAKE CHICKEN

Cornflakes make the best coating for chicken. The flavor is far better than plain bread crumbs, and it gives the chicken a nice crunch, especially if you double-bread it.
—*Angela Capettini, Boynton Beach, FL*

PREP: 10 MIN. • COOK: 20 MIN. • MAKES: 4 SERVINGS

1 cup crushed cornflakes
1 cup all-purpose flour
1½ tsp. seasoned salt
¾ cup egg substitute
4 chicken drumsticks
   (4 oz. each), skin removed
4 bone-in chicken
   thighs (about 1½ lbs.),
   skin removed
   Cooking spray

1. Preheat air fryer to 400°. In a shallow bowl, combine the cornflakes, flour and seasoned salt. Place egg substitute in another shallow bowl. Dip chicken in egg substitute, then roll in cornflake mixture. Repeat.

2. In batches, arrange chicken drumsticks on greased tray in air-fryer basket, meatier side down; spritz liberally with cooking spray. Cook until a thermometer reads 170°-175°, roughly 20-30 minutes, turning occasionally.

1 drumstick and 1 thigh: 494 cal., 13g fat (3g sat. fat), 128mg chol., 931mg sod., 44g carb. (2g sugars, 1g fiber), 47g pro.

CHAPTER 7

BEEF ENTREES

When you want to add vigor and heartiness to a home-cooked meal, reach for the beef. It is, after all, the most popular solution to any night's "What's for dinner?" conundrum, and these savory air-fried entrees—including sizzling steaks, comforting ground beef and other meaty favorites—are sure to satisfy.

STUFFED ZUCCHINI

Is your garden overflowing with zucchini? Pull out your air fryer! Filled with ground beef and cheese, this quick-to-fix meal is a delicious way to enjoy summer's bounty.

—Tracey Rosato, Markham, ON

PREP: 20 MIN. • COOK: 15 MIN. • MAKES: 4 SERVINGS

2 large zucchini
1 lb. ground beef
1 garlic clove, minced
1 cup shredded Havarti cheese with jalapeno or Havarti cheese
¾ cup crumbled feta cheese, divided
2 Tbsp. minced fresh basil or oregano
¼ tsp. salt
⅛ tsp. pepper

1. Cut each zucchini in half lengthwise; cut a thin slice from the bottoms so they sit flat. Scoop out pulp, leaving ¼-in. shells.

2. In a large cast-iron or other heavy skillet over medium heat, cook beef and garlic until meat is no longer pink; drain. Stir in Havarti cheese, ½ cup feta cheese, basil, salt and pepper.

3. Preheat air fryer to 350°. Fill zucchini with meat mixture. Place on greased tray in air-fryer basket. Cook 8 minutes. Top with remaining ¼ cup feta; cook until zucchini is tender and cheese is melted, about 5 minutes.

1 stuffed zucchini half: 390 cal., 26g fat (13g sat. fat), 108mg chol., 583mg sod., 6g carb. (4g sugars, 2g fiber), 32g pro.

ROAST BEEF WITH HORSERADISH SAUCE

This recipe turns an inexpensive cut of beef into a delicious main dish. And the air fryer cuts the roasting time, so I don't feel bad making it on a weeknight.
—*Rita Drewes, Craig, MO*

PREP: 10 MIN. • COOK: 35 MIN. + STANDING • MAKES: 8 SERVINGS

¼ cup dry bread crumbs
2 Tbsp. olive oil
1 garlic clove, minced
1 tsp. ground mustard
1 tsp. dried savory
1 tsp. pepper
½ tsp. dried rosemary, crushed
1 boneless beef chuck or top blade roast (about 3 lbs.)

SAUCE
1 cup sour cream
3 Tbsp. prepared horseradish
1 tsp. lemon juice
¼ tsp. salt

1. Preheat air fryer to 375° for 10-15 minutes. In a bowl, combine the first 7 ingredients. Rub over entire roast. Place on greased tray in air-fryer basket. Cook 20 minutes; flip roast. Reduce heat to 325°, cook until meat reaches desired degree of doneness (for medium-rare, a thermometer should read 135°; medium, 140°; medium-well, 145°), 15-25 minutes. Let stand 20 minutes before carving.

2. Meanwhile, in a bowl, combine all sauce ingredients. Serve with roast.

6 oz.-weight: 394 cal., 25g fat (10g sat. fat), 129mg chol., 205mg sod., 5g carb. (1g sugars, 0 fiber), 35g pro.

HEARTY MEAT LOAF

Here's a homestyle entree that's perfect for two. This small-scale meat loaf cooks quickly in the air fryer. It's easy to double for sandwiches the next day.
—*Michelle Beran, Claflin, KS*

PREP: 15 MIN. • BAKE: 30 MIN. • MAKES: 2 MINI MEAT LOAVES

1 large egg
¼ cup 2% milk
⅓ cup crushed saltines
3 Tbsp. chopped onion
¼ tsp. salt
⅛ tsp. rubbed sage
   Dash pepper
½ lb. lean ground
   beef (90% lean)
¼ cup ketchup
2 Tbsp. brown sugar
¼ tsp. Worcestershire sauce

1. In a large bowl, beat egg. Add the milk, cracker crumbs, onion, salt, sage and pepper. Crumble beef over mixture and mix lightly but thoroughly. Preheat air fryer to 325°. Shape into 2 loaves; place on greased tray in air-fryer basket. Cook 20 minutes.

2. Meanwhile, in a bowl, combine ketchup, brown sugar and Worcestershire sauce; spoon over meat loaves. Cook until a thermometer reads 160°, 10-15 minutes longer.

1 serving: 337 cal., 12g fat (4g sat. fat), 162mg chol., 898mg sod., 31g carb. (18g sugars, 1g fiber), 27g pro. **Diabetic exchanges:** 3 lean meat, 2 starch.

AIR-FRYING TIP
The easiest way to keep meat loaf juicy is to not slice it right away. Let it rest for about 10 minutes before serving.

BEEF TURNOVERS

My mom's recipe for these flavorful pockets called for dough made from scratch, but I streamlined it by using refrigerated crescent rolls and an air fryer. My children love the turnovers plain or dipped in ketchup.
—*Claudia Bodeker, Ash Flat, AR*

TAKES: 30 MIN. • MAKES: 1 DOZEN

1 lb. ground beef
1 medium onion, chopped
1 jar (16 oz.) sauerkraut, rinsed, drained and chopped
1 cup shredded Swiss cheese
3 tubes (8 oz. each) refrigerated crescent rolls

1. In a large skillet, cook beef and onion over medium heat until meat is no longer pink, 5-7 minutes; crumble meat; drain. Add sauerkraut and cheese.

2. Preheat air fryer to 350°. Unroll the crescent roll dough and separate into rectangles; pinch seams to seal. Place ½ cup beef mixture in the center of each rectangle. Bring corners to the center and pinch to seal. In batches, place turnovers in a single layer on greased tray in air-fryer basket. Cook until golden brown, 12-15 minutes.

2 turnovers: 634 cal., 35g fat (7g sat. fat), 63mg chol., 1426mg sod., 54g carb. (14g sugars, 2g fiber), 27g pro.

COWBOY CASSEROLE

When the weather turns cold, I make this quick and easy Tater Tot bake.
I assemble the small casserole ahead of time and keep it in the refrigerator.
Then I just pop it in the air fryer when I get home.
—*Donna Donhauser, Remsen, NY*

TAKES: 30 MIN. • MAKES: 2 SERVINGS

½ lb. lean ground
  beef (90% lean)
1 can (8¾ oz.) whole
  kernel corn, drained
⅔ cup condensed cream of
  chicken soup, undiluted
½ cup shredded cheddar
  cheese, divided
⅓ cup 2% milk
2 Tbsp. sour cream
¾ tsp. onion powder
¼ tsp. pepper
2 cups frozen Tater Tots

1. In a large skillet, cook beef over medium heat until no longer pink. Stir in corn, soup, ¼ cup cheese, milk, sour cream, onion powder and pepper.

2. Preheat air fryer to 350°. Place 1 cup Tater Tots in a greased 3-cup baking dish that fits into your air fryer. Layer with beef mixture and remaining 1 cup Tater Tots; sprinkle with remaining ¼ cup cheese. Cook, uncovered, until bubbly, 15-20 minutes.

1 serving: 714 cal., 38g fat (15g sat. fat), 120mg chol., 1675mg sod., 56g carb. (9g sugars, 6g fiber), 37g pro.

WHY YOU'LL LOVE IT...
"This is the kind of recipe I like the most—quick, easy and yummy."
—CWEISE, TASTEOFHOME.COM

STUFFED PEPPERS

My mother came from a family of fantastic Cajun cooks, so our food was always well-seasoned. In Louisiana, rice is part of many meals. The cheese sauce sets these stuffed peppers apart from any others I've tried.

—Lisa Easley, Longview, TX

PREP: 40 MIN. • COOK: 10 MIN. • MAKES: 4 SERVINGS

1 lb. ground beef
1 small onion, chopped
1 small green pepper, chopped
1 garlic clove, minced
½ tsp. salt
¼ tsp. pepper
2 cups water
⅔ cup diced tomatoes with mild green chiles
1 can (8 oz.) tomato sauce
1½ tsp. ground cumin
1½ cups uncooked instant rice
2 medium green peppers

CHEESE SAUCE
¾ lb. Velveeta, cubed
⅔ cup diced tomatoes with mild green chiles

1. In a large skillet, cook the beef, onion, chopped green pepper, garlic, cumin, salt and pepper over medium heat until beef is no longer pink; drain. Add water, tomatoes and tomato sauce. Bring to a boil. Reduce heat; simmer, uncovered, for 10 minutes.

2. Stir in rice; simmer, uncovered, for 5 minutes. Remove from heat; cover and let stand for 5 minutes.

3. Preheat air fryer to 325°. Remove the tops and seeds from peppers; cut in half. Place on greased tray in air-fryer basket. Cook until almost tender, 4-5 minutes.

4. Stuff peppers with meat mixture. Return peppers to air fryer; cook until heated through and the peppers are tender, roughly 10-12 minutes.

5. Meanwhile, in a saucepan over medium heat, stir sauce ingredients until melted. Serve cheese sauce over peppers.

1 stuffed pepper half: 689 cal., 36g fat (18g sat. fat), 153mg chol., 1918mg sod., 51g carb. (11g sugars, 5g fiber), 40g pro.

BACON-WRAPPED FILETS

I got the idea for bacon-wrapped filet mignon when I saw some on sale
in the grocery store. The rest was inspired by my husband, because
he once made a Scotch and ginger ale sauce. I originally made
this in the oven but it works equally well in the air fryer.
—*Mary Kay LaBrie, Clermont, FL*

TAKES: 30 MIN. • MAKES: 2 SERVINGS

2 bacon strips
2 beef tenderloin
   steaks (5 oz. each)
¼ tsp. salt
¼ tsp. coarsely ground pepper
2 cups sliced baby
   portobello mushrooms
¼ tsp. dried thyme
2 Tbsp. butter, divided
1½ tsp. olive oil
¼ cup Scotch whiskey
½ cup diet ginger ale
1 Tbsp. brown sugar
1½ tsp. reduced-sodium
   soy sauce
¼ tsp. rubbed sage

1. Place bacon in a single layer in air-fryer basket. Cook at 350°
until partially cooked but not crisp, roughly 3-4 minutes. Remove
to paper towels to drain.

2. Preheat air fryer to 375°. Sprinkle steaks with salt and pepper;
wrap a strip of bacon around the side of each steak and secure
with toothpicks. Place steaks in a single layer in air fryer. Cook
until the meat reaches desired doneness (for medium-rare, a
thermometer should read 135°; medium, 140°; medium-well,
145°), 7-10 minutes, turning halfway through.

3. Meanwhile, in a large skillet, saute mushrooms and thyme in
1 Tbsp. butter and oil until tender; remove from heat. Add the
whiskey, stirring to loosen browned bits from pan. Stir in ginger
ale, brown sugar, soy sauce and sage.

4. Bring to a boil. Reduce heat; simmer, uncovered, until liquid is
reduced by half, 3-5 minutes. Stir in the remaining Tbsp. butter.
Serve mushrooms with steaks.

1 filet with ⅓ cup mushroom mixture: 581 cal., 37 g fat (15 g sat. fat), 108 mg chol.,
729 mg sod., 10 g carb. (8 g sugars, 1 g fiber), 35 g pro.

EASY SALISBURY STEAK

This classic dish can be made in 30 minutes or less, making it the perfect weeknight meal. I often double the recipe and freeze one batch of cooked steaks and gravy for an even faster meal on an especially busy night.

—*Carol Callahan, Rome, GA*

TAKES: 30 MIN. • MAKES: 4 SERVINGS

⅓ cup chopped onion
¼ cup crushed saltines
1 egg white, lightly beaten
2 Tbsp. 2% milk
1 Tbsp. prepared horseradish
¼ tsp. salt, optional
⅛ tsp. pepper
1 lb. lean ground beef (90% lean)
1 jar (12 oz.) beef gravy
1½ cups sliced fresh mushrooms
2 Tbsp. water
Hot cooked noodles, optional

1. Preheat air fryer to 350° for 5-10 minutes. In a large bowl, combine onion, saltines, egg white, milk, horseradish, salt if desired, and pepper. Crumble beef over mixture. Shape into 4 oval patties. Place patties on greased tray in air-fryer basket. Cook until browned and thermometer reads 160°, 12-15 minutes, turning once.

2. Meanwhile, in a large skillet, stir together gravy, mushrooms and water; cook over medium high heat until heated through, 3-5 minutes. Serve with patties and noodles if desired.

1 serving: 253 cal., 11g fat (4g sat. fat), 78mg chol., 582mg sod., 11g carb. (2g sugars, 1g fiber), 26g pro. **Diabetic exchanges:** 3 lean meat, ½ starch.

WHY YOU'LL LOVE IT...
"Fabulous flavor! Definitely loved the horseradish addition. Made it for dinner tonight with the onions and mushrooms on the side and used bread crumbs instead of saltines, no additional salt. Kids loved it over mashed potatoes and with broccoli... great dinner for the family."
—FRITZTIGER2000, TASTEOFHOME.COM

TACO KABOBS

We typically think of the grill when making kabobs but an air fryer does
an equally good job in the same amount of time. Sometimes I'll add a drop or
two of liquid smoke to the marinade to give it that grilled flavor.

—Dixie Terry, Goreville, IL

PREP: 15 MIN. + MARINATING • COOK: 10 MIN. • MAKES: 6 SERVINGS

1 envelope taco seasoning
1 cup tomato juice
2 Tbsp. canola oil
2 lbs. beef top sirloin steak,
  cut into 1-in. cubes
1 medium green pepper,
  cut into chunks
1 medium sweet red
  pepper, cut into chunks
1 large onion, cut into wedges
12 cherry tomatoes
  Optional: Salsa con queso
  or sour cream

1. In a large shallow dish, combine taco seasoning, tomato juice and oil; mix well. Remove ½ cup for basting; refrigerate. Add the beef to shallow dish and turn to coat. Cover; refrigerate at least 5 hours.

2. Preheat air fryer to 400° for 10 minutes. Drain and discard marinade from beef. On 6 metal or soaked wooden skewers that fit in your air fryer, alternately thread beef, peppers, onion and tomatoes. In batches, place skewers in a single layer on greased tray in air-fryer basket. Cook, turning and basting occasionally with reserved marinade, until meat reaches desired doneness, 8-10 minutes. Serve with salsa con queso or sour cream if desired.

1 kabob: 277 cal., 10g fat (3g sat. fat), 61mg chol., 665mg sod., 12g carb. (4g sugars, 2g fiber), 34g pro. **Diabetic exchanges:** 4 lean meat, 2 vegetable, 1 fat.

CHICKEN-FRIED STEAKS

There's nothing more comforting and down-home than a good chicken-fried steak.
An air fryer does a great job cooking delicious foods with less fat and fewer calories.
Take one bite of this and you'll agree!
—*Denice Louk, Garnett, KS*

PREP: 15 MIN. • COOK: 15 MIN./BATCH • MAKES: 4 SERVINGS

2 cups all-purpose
   flour, divided
2 tsp. baking powder
¾ tsp. each salt, onion
   powder, garlic powder,
   chili powder and pepper
1 large egg, lightly beaten
1¼ cups buttermilk, divided
4 beef cubed steaks
   (4 oz. each)
   Cooking spray
⅓ cup canola oil
1½ cups 2% milk

1. In a shallow bowl, combine 1¾ cups flour, baking powder and seasonings. In another shallow bowl, combine egg and ¾ cup buttermilk. Dip each cube steak in buttermilk mixture, then roll in flour mixture. Let stand for 5 minutes.

2. Preheat air fryer to 375°. In batches, place steaks in a single layer on greased tray in air-fryer basket; spritz with cooking spray. Cook for 6 minutes. Turn carefully; spritz with cooking spray. Cook until coating is crisp and meat is no longer pink, 5-6 minutes longer.

3. Meanwhile, in a saucepan, stir together oil and remaining ¼ cup flour until smooth. Cook and stir over medium heat for 2 minutes. Gradually whisk in the milk and remaining ½ cup buttermilk. Bring to a boil; cook and stir until thickened, roughly 2 minutes. Serve gravy with steaks.

1 steak with ½ cup gravy: 400 cal., 8g fat (3g sat. fat), 88mg chol., 896mg sod., 45g carb. (8g sugars, 2g fiber), 36g pro.

BEEF JERKY

Jerky is a portable, chewy snack you can easily make in your air fryer. This version has a savory teriyaki flavor and a bit of heat, but feel free to reduce the pepper flakes.
—Taste of Home *Test Kitchen*

PREP: 40 MIN. + MARINATING • COOK: 1¾ HOURS • MAKES: 8 SERVINGS

1 beef flank steak
   (1½ to 2 lbs.)
⅔ cup reduced-sodium
   soy sauce
⅔ cup Worcestershire sauce
¼ cup honey
3 tsp. coarsely ground pepper
2 tsp. onion powder
2 tsp. garlic powder
1½ tsp. crushed red
   pepper flakes
1 tsp. liquid smoke

1. Trim all visible fat from steak. Freeze, covered, 30 minutes or until firm. Slice steak along the grain into long ⅛-in.-thick strips.

2. Transfer to a shallow dish. In a small bowl, whisk remaining ingredients; add to the beef. Turn to coat. Refrigerate, covered, 2 hours or overnight, turning occasionally.

3. Preheat air fryer to 350°. Drain beef, discarding marinade. In batches, arrange beef strips in single layer on greased tray in air-fryer basket. Cook until meat reaches 165°. Reduce heat to 175°. Cook until desired texture is achieved, 1½-2 hours.

4. Remove from air fryer; cool completely on wire racks. Using paper towels, blot any beads of oil on jerky. For best quality and longer storage, store jerky, covered, in refrigerator or freezer.

1 oz.: 132 cal., 6g fat (3g sat. fat), 40mg chol., 139mg sod., 2g carb. (1g sugars, 0 fiber), 17g pro.

WHY YOU'LL LOVE IT...
"Great recipe. I tweaked it a little by putting my own touch on it. I added brown sugar and a teaspoon of horseradish."
—OZRKCRAFTER, TASTEOFHOME.COM

AIR-FRYING TIP

Serve these puffs with sliced jalapenos, pico de gallo or any of your favorite taco toppings, such as shredded or crumbled cheese, lettuce, onions, bell peppers, avocado, cilantro, sour cream or salsa.

TACO PUFFS

I make these puffs ahead of time and keep them in the refrigerator until I'm ready to pop them in the air fryer. A helpful hint: Plain refrigerated biscuits seal together better than buttermilk types.
—*Jan Schmid, Hibbing, MN*

PREP: 15 MIN. • COOK: 10 MIN./BATCH • MAKES: 8 SERVINGS

1 lb. ground beef
½ cup chopped onion
1 envelope taco seasoning
2 tubes (16.3 oz. each) large refrigerated flaky biscuits
2 cups shredded cheddar cheese

1. In a large skillet, cook beef and onion over medium heat until meat is no longer pink, 5-7 minutes, breaking into crumbles; drain. Add taco seasoning and prepare according to package directions. Cool slightly.

2. Preheat air fryer to 350°. Flatten half the biscuits into 4-in. circles. Spoon ¼ cup meat mixture onto each circle; sprinkle each with ¼ cup cheese. Flatten remaining biscuits; place over filling and pinch edges to seal tightly.

3. In batches, place puffs in a single layer on greased tray in air-fryer basket. Cook until golden brown and puffed, 10-15 minutes.

1 taco puff: 574 cal., 28g fat (13g sat. fat), 63mg chol., 1538mg sod., 55g carb. (9g sugars, 0 fiber), 23g pro.

CHAPTER 8

SANDWICHES

Whether it's a sizzling burger, a melty grilled cheese
or a fork-tender meat filling piled high on a bun,
a hot sandwich can be a simple, cozy meal.
Prepare to be amazed when you rely on your handy
air fryer to kick up your sandwich game!

STUFFED PORK BURGERS

Mix ground beef and pork for burgers that are out of this world.
Stuffing them takes a bit of extra time, but it's well worth it!
—*Francine Lizotte, Surrey, BC*

PREP: 30 MIN. + CHILLING • COOK: 10 MIN. • MAKES: 6 SERVINGS

1 lb. ground beef
1 lb. ground pork
¼ cup panko bread crumbs
¼ cup finely chopped
   red onion
4½ tsp. minced fresh basil
1 tsp. smoked paprika
¼ tsp. salt
¼ tsp. pepper
6 Tbsp. finely chopped
   fresh pineapple
6 Tbsp. barbecue sauce
6 bacon strips, cooked
   and crumbled
   Sliced Jarlsberg cheese,
   optional
6 hamburger buns, split

1. In a large bowl, combine the first 8 ingredients, mixing lightly but thoroughly. Shape into 12 thin patties. Divide pineapple, barbecue sauce and bacon over center of 6 patties; top with remaining patties, pressing edges firmly to seal. Refrigerate, covered, for 1 hour.

2. Preheat air fryer to 350°. In batches, arrange patties in a single layer on greased tray in air-fryer basket. Cook until thermometer reads 160°, 8-10 minutes turning once. If desired, top with cheese. Serve on buns and, if desired, top with additional barbecue sauce, red onion and fresh basil.

1 burger: 508 cal., 25g fat (9g sat. fat), 105mg chol., 724mg sod., 33g carb. (10g sugars, 1g fiber), 35g pro.

AIR-FRYING TIP

If you like the signature spicy mayo served on some fast-food chain chicken sandwiches, you'll love how easy it is to replicate it at home. Simply mix together mayonnaise and your favorite hot pepper sauce, adjusted to whatever heat level you prefer.

COPYCAT FRIED CHICKEN SANDWICH

After trying all the major fast food chain's chicken sandwiches, I decided to come up with my own. I think mine is better than all the restaurant versions. Give it a try—I bet you'll agree!
—*Ralph Jones, San Diego, CA*

PREP: 15 MIN. + MARINATING • COOK: 20 MIN./BATCH • MAKES: 6 SERVINGS

3 boneless skinless chicken breast halves (6 oz. each)
¾ cup buttermilk
2 tsp. hot pepper sauce
2 large eggs, beaten
2 cups all-purpose flour
1 Tbsp. plus 1 tsp. garlic powder
1 Tbsp. each onion powder and paprika
2 tsp. pepper
1 tsp. salt
⅓ cup canola oil
6 brioche hamburger buns, split
   Optional: Shredded lettuce, sliced tomatoes, pickle slices, onion slices, mayonnaise

1. Cut each chicken breast horizontally in half; place in a large bowl. Add buttermilk and hot sauce; toss to coat. Refrigerate, covered, 8 hours or overnight.

2. Preheat air fryer to 400°. Stir eggs into chicken mixture. In a shallow dish, whisk flour, garlic powder, onion powder, paprika, pepper and salt. Remove the chicken from buttermilk mixture. Dredge chicken in flour mixture, firmly patting to help coating adhere. Repeat, dipping chicken again in buttermilk mixture and then dredging in flour mixture.

3. Place chicken on a wire rack over a baking sheet. Refrigerate, uncovered, for 30 minutes. Using a pastry brush, lightly dab both sides of chicken with oil until no dry breading remains.

4. In batches, arrange the chicken in a single layer on greased tray in air-fryer basket. Cook until a thermometer reads 165° and coating is golden brown and crispy, 7-8 minutes on each side. Remove chicken; keep warm. Toast buns in air fryer until golden brown, 2-3 minutes. Top bun bottoms with chicken. If desired, serve with optional toppings.

1 sandwich: 384 cal., 17g fat (3g sat. fat), 136mg chol., 777mg sod., 31g carb. (8g sugars, 3g fiber), 26g pro.

BRATWURST SANDWICHES WITH BEER GRAVY

These brats are a nod to my German heritage. I serve them with a green vegetable and french fries or mashed potatoes on the side. For a deeper sauce flavor, use a lager or stout beer.
—*Allison Ochoa, Hays, KS*

TAKES: 20 MIN. • MAKES: 5 SERVINGS

1 pkg. uncooked bratwurst links (20 oz.)
2 Tbsp. butter
1 medium onion, thinly sliced
2 Tbsp. all-purpose flour
⅛ tsp. dill weed
⅛ tsp. pepper
1 bottle (12 oz.) beer or nonalcoholic beer
5 slices thick bread

1. Preheat air fryer to 400°. Place bratwurst in a single layer on greased tray in air-fryer basket. Cook until no longer pink, 8-10 minutes.

2. Meanwhile, in a large saucepan, heat butter over medium-high heat. Add onion; cook and stir until onions start to brown and soften. Add flour, dill weed and pepper; stir until smooth. Stir in beer. Bring to a boil. Reduce heat; simmer, stirring constantly until thickened, 3-5 minutes. To serve, place 1 brat on each slice of bread; top evenly with onion mixture.

1 bratwurst sandwich with ¼ cup gravy: 526 cal., 39g fat (14g sat. fat), 96mg chol., 1140mg sod., 23g carb. (3g sugars, 1g fiber), 19g pro.

CHEESY QUESADILLAS

I cut these into small triangles and serve them as party appetizers. They're also wonderful dipped in chili or sour cream. Feel free to switch up the cheese and the salsa to suit your taste.

—Terri Keeney, Greeley, CO

TAKES: 10 MIN. • MAKES: 6 SERVINGS

1½ cups shredded Mexican
    cheese blend
½ cup salsa
4 flour tortillas
    (8 in.), warmed
    Cooking spray

Preheat air fryer to 375°. Combine cheese and salsa; spread over half of each tortilla. Fold tortilla over. In batches, place tortillas in a single layer on greased tray in air-fryer basket; spritz with cooking spray. Cook until golden brown and cheese has melted, roughly 5-7 minutes. Cut into wedges.

1 serving: 223 cal., 11g fat (5g sat. fat), 25mg chol., 406mg sod., 21g carb. (1g sugars, 1g fiber), 9g pro.

WHY YOU'LL LOVE IT...
"I am 13, and made this all by myself for my family of six. They all loved it!"
—GUEST8518, TASTEOFHOME.COM

GENERAL TSO'S CHICKEN SANDWICH WITH BROCCOLI SLAW

I turned a classic takeout dinner into a sandwich that's simple to make at home. The air fryer keeps it lighter but still crunchy, and the recipe can be made in under 30 minutes, which is a must for our active family. We like spicy foods, so this sauce has a good amount of heat.
—*Julie Peterson, Crofton, MD*

PREP: 30 MIN. • COOK: 10 MIN./BATCH • MAKES: 4 SERVINGS

½ cup reduced-fat mayonnaise
2 Tbsp. honey
1 Tbsp. rice vinegar
2 tsp. hoisin sauce
3 cups broccoli coleslaw mix
½ cup sliced almonds
1 lb. boneless skinless chicken thighs, cut into ½-in. strips
4 Tbsp. cornstarch
½ tsp. salt
¼ tsp. pepper

SAUCE
¼ cup hoisin sauce
3 Tbsp. reduced-sodium soy sauce
3 Tbsp. honey
1 Tbsp. minced fresh gingerroot
2 garlic cloves, minced
½ to 1 tsp. crushed red pepper flakes
4 brioche hamburger buns, split
Sesame seeds

1. In a large bowl, combine the mayonnaise, honey, vinegar and hoisin sauce. Stir in coleslaw mix and almonds; refrigerate until serving.

2. Preheat air fryer to 400°. Toss chicken with cornstarch, salt and pepper. In batches, arrange the chicken in a single layer on greased tray in air-fryer basket. Cook until lightly browned and chicken is no longer pink, 4-5 minutes on each side.

3. Meanwhile, in a small saucepan, combine hoisin sauce, soy sauce, honey, ginger, garlic and pepper flakes; bring to a boil. Reduce heat; simmer, uncovered, until sauce thickens, about 5 minutes. Add cooked chicken; toss to coat.

4. Spoon chicken on bun bottoms; top with coleslaw mix and sprinkle with sesame seeds. Replace tops.

1 sandwich: 678 cal., 29g fat (5g sat. fat), 117mg chol., 1587mg sod., 75g carb. (37g sugars, 6g fiber), 32g pro.

AIR FRYING TIP
Want even more olives?
Finely chop ½ cup and add
to the beef mixture before
forming into patties.

MOM'S OLIVE BURGERS

My mom would reminisce about the olive burgers she would get at Coney Island when she was a girl. After a little trial and error, I made her a version that was just like the ones she remembered.
—*Lorraine Hickman, Lansing, MI*

TAKES: 25 MIN. • MAKES: 4 SERVINGS

1 lb. ground beef
2 tsp. reduced-sodium soy sauce
2 tsp. Worcestershire sauce
¼ tsp. garlic powder
¼ tsp. onion powder
½ cup sliced green olives with pimientos, drained
¼ cup Miracle Whip or mayonnaise
1 Tbsp. stone-ground mustard
4 hamburger buns, toasted
¼ cup crumbled feta cheese, optional
   Bibb lettuce leaves, optional

1. In a large bowl, combine the beef, soy sauce, Worcestershire, garlic powder and onion powder, mixing lightly but thoroughly. Shape into four ½-in.-thick patties, indenting the center slightly.

2. Preheat air fryer to 350°. Arrange patties in a single layer on greased tray in air-fryer basket. Cook until a thermometer reads 160°, roughly 8-10 minutes turning once.

3. Meanwhile, in a small bowl combine olives, Miracle Whip and mustard. Serve burgers on buns with olive mixture. If desired, top with feta cheese and lettuce.

1 burger with 2 Tbsp. olive mixture: 400 cal., 21g fat (6g sat. fat), 75mg chol., 814mg sod., 26g carb. (5g sugars, 1g fiber), 25g pro.

HOISIN CHICKEN WRAPS

I was inspired by the iconic Vietnamese banh mi sandwich, particularly the fresh carrot, cucumber and radish topping. It adds so much fresh flavor, color and crunch!
—*Debbie Glasscock, Conway, AR*

PREP: 25 MIN. + MARINATING • COOK: 10 MIN. • MAKES: 6 SERVINGS

⅓ cup hoisin sauce
¼ cup reduced-sodium soy sauce
3 Tbsp. brown sugar, divided
2 Tbsp. lime juice
2 garlic cloves, minced
6 chicken tenderloins (about ¾ lb.)
2 Tbsp. rice vinegar
¼ tsp. Sriracha chili sauce, divided
1 cup julienned carrots
1 cup julienned radishes
½ cup mayonnaise
1 tsp. honey
6 flour tortillas (10 in.), room temperature
4 miniature cucumbers, cut into thin ribbons
Fresh mint or basil leaves

1. In a small bowl or shallow dish, combine hoisin sauce, soy sauce, 2 Tbsp. brown sugar, lime juice and garlic. Add chicken; turn to coat. Refrigerate 30 minutes.

2. Meanwhile, in a large bowl, whisk vinegar, ⅛ tsp. Sriracha and remaining 1 Tbsp. brown sugar. Add carrots and radishes; toss to coat. Set aside.

3. Preheat air fryer to 400°. Drain chicken, discarding marinade; pat dry with paper towels. Arrange chicken in a single layer on greased tray in air-fryer basket; cook until a thermometer reads 165°, roughly 4-5 minutes on each side. Remove to a cutting board; cool slightly. Slice chicken into ½-in. pieces.

4. Combine mayonnaise, honey and remaining ⅛ tsp. Sriracha; spread over tortillas. Layer with the chicken, carrot mixture, cucumber and mint. Fold bottom and sides of tortilla over filling and roll up.

1 wrap: 439 cal., 20g fat (4g sat. fat), 35mg chol., 828mg sod., 46g carb. (11g sugars, 4g fiber), 20g pro.

ASIAN TURKEY BURGER WITH APPLE SLAW

I wanted to give my turkey burgers a bit of an Asian flair. On a whim, I added hoisin sauce, ginger and garlic. We love this version so much, we now eat them at least once a week.

—*Ashley Gayle, Ellicott City, MD*

TAKES: 25 MIN. • MAKES: 4 SERVINGS

3 green onions, finely chopped
2 Tbsp. hoisin sauce
1 Tbsp. minced fresh gingerroot
2 garlic cloves, minced
½ tsp. salt
¼ tsp. pepper
1¼ lbs. ground turkey

SLAW
3 Tbsp. olive oil
1 Tbsp. cider vinegar
1 tsp. Dijon mustard
¼ tsp. salt
⅛ tsp. pepper
2 medium apples, julienned
2 green onions, finely chopped

ASSEMBLY
4 hamburger buns, split and toasted
2 Tbsp. hoisin sauce

1. Preheat air fryer to 350°. In a large bowl, mix green onions, hoisin sauce, ginger, garlic, salt and pepper. Add turkey; mix lightly but thoroughly. Shape into four ¾-in.-thick patties.

2. Place burgers in a single layer on greased tray in air-fryer basket. Cook until a thermometer reads 165°, 5-6 minutes on each side.

3. Meanwhile, for slaw, in a large bowl, whisk oil, vinegar, mustard, salt and pepper. Add apples and green onions; toss to coat.

4. To assemble, spread bun bottoms with hoisin sauce. Top with burgers and slaw; replace tops.

Freeze option: Place patties on a foil-lined baking sheet, wrap and freeze until firm. Remove from pan and transfer to a freezer container; return to freezer. To use, cook the frozen patties as directed, increasing cook time as necessary for a thermometer to read 165°.

1 burger with 1 cup apple slaw: 502 cal., 23g fat (5g sat. fat), 94mg chol., 1031mg sod., 42g carb. (16g sugars, 4g fiber), 33g pro.

GRILLED CHEESE SANDWICHES

The air fryer is a genius way to make these golden, toasty sandwiches. The hot circulated air gets the cheese more gooey and melty than a stovetop griddle. If I'm only making one, I'll also pop a few frozen fries in with the sandwich.
—*Edie DeSpain, Logan, UT*

TAKES: 15 MIN. • MAKES: 2 SERVINGS

2 Tbsp. mayonnaise
1 tsp. Dijon mustard
4 slices sourdough bread
2 slices Swiss cheese
2 slices cheddar cheese
2 slices sweet onion
1 medium tomato, sliced
6 cooked bacon strips
2 Tbsp. butter, softened

1. Preheat air fryer to 375°. Combine mayonnaise and mustard; spread over 2 bread slices. Layer with cheeses, onion, tomato and bacon; top with the remaining bread. Spread outsides of sandwiches with butter.

2. Place sandwiches in a single layer in tray in air fryer basket. Cook until cheese is melted, 2-3 minutes on each side.

1 sandwich: 639 cal., 47g fat (21g sat. fat), 110mg chol., 1266mg sod., 28g carb. (4g sugars, 2g fiber), 27g pro.

TEST KITCHEN TIP: If your bread starts to get too dark before the cheese is fully melted, consider turning the temperature down a bit. Also, flipping the sandwich halfway through should help the heat distribute evenly for the perfect sandwich.

PECAN CHICKEN SLIDERS

I love coating chicken in pecans instead of breadcrumbs because it gives you such a wonderful crunch and flavor. If you don't have an air fryer you can bake them in the oven for the same taste.

—Amy Freeze, Avon Park, FL

PREP: 30 MIN. • COOK: 10 MIN./BATCH • MAKES: 2 DOZEN

12 small boneless skinless chicken thighs (about 2 lbs.)
4 cups finely chopped pecans
1 large egg, beaten
¼ cup 2% milk
1 tsp. salt
1 tsp. pepper
2-3 dashes hot pepper sauce, such as Tabasco
Cooking spray

BOURBON BERRY JAM
1 pkg. (16 oz.) frozen unsweetened mixed berries
1 cup sugar
⅓ cup bourbon
¼ cup cornstarch

SLAW
1 pkg. (16 oz.) tri-color coleslaw mix
½ cup mayonnaise
3 Tbsp. sugar
3 Tbsp. lime juice
2 pkg. (12 oz. each) Hawaiian sweet rolls, split

1. Preheat air fryer to 375°. Flatten chicken to ½-in. thickness; cut each thigh in half. Place pecans in a shallow dish. In another shallow dish, whisk together egg, milk, salt, pepper and pepper sauce. Dip chicken in egg mixture, then coat with pecans. In batches, arrange chicken in a single layer on greased tray in air-fryer basket; spritz with cooking spray. Cook until golden brown, turning once, 8-10 minutes.

2. Meanwhile, combine the jam ingredients in a saucepan over medium-high heat. Bring to a boil, reduce heat and simmer until thick, 1-2 minutes. Remove from heat; crush berries to desired consistency. For slaw, in a large bowl, combine the coleslaw mix, mayonnaise, sugar and lime juice. To assemble, spoon 1 heaping Tbsp. jam onto bottom of each roll. Layer with hot chicken and slaw; replace tops.

1 slider: 335 cal., 18g fat (4g sat. fat), 42mg chol., 228mg sod., 33g carb. (19g sugars, 3g fiber), 11g pro.

TAILGATE SAUSAGES

I love these sausages, not only for their fantastic taste, but also because I can make them ahead of time and keep them refrigerated until it's time to cook.
—*Matthew Hass, Ellison Bay, WI*

TAKES: 20 MIN. • MAKES: 4 SERVINGS

4 slices provolone cheese
4 brat buns or hot
   dog buns, split
4 cooked Italian sausage links
½ cup giardiniera, drained

AIR-FRYING TIP
Giardiniera is a medley of pickled vegetables, most commonly cauliflower, carrots, celery, onions, bell peppers and serrano or jalapeno peppers. It's often eaten as a condiment on sausages, hot dogs or Italian beef sandwiches.

Preheat air fryer to 350°. Place cheese in buns; top with Italian sausages and giardiniera. Wrap individually in heavy-duty foil (about 12x10 in.). Place in a single layer in air fryer. Cook until heated through and cheese is melted, 8-10 minutes. Open foil carefully to allow steam to escape. If desired, serve sausages with additional giardiniera.

1 sandwich: 574 cal., 33g fat (12g sat. fat), 62mg chol., 1542mg sod., 40g carb. (7g sugars, 1g fiber), 29g pro.

MASALA CHICKEN SANDWICHES

Reaching back to my Indian roots, I created this recipe with a modern twist.
I add a half or a whole serrano pepper to the slaw for a little extra kick.
—*Mary Lou Timpson, Centennial Park, AZ*

PREP: 30 MIN. + MARINATING • COOK: 20 MIN. • MAKES: 4 SERVINGS

2 Tbsp. plain Greek yogurt
2 Tbsp. tandoori
  masala seasoning
4 boneless skinless chicken
  thighs (about 1 lb.)

SLAW
1 cup shredded daikon radish
2 Tbsp. grated onion
2 Tbsp. lime juice
2 Tbsp. minced fresh cilantro
¼ tsp. salt

SAUCE
½ cup plain Greek yogurt
2 Tbsp. minced fresh mint
1 Tbsp. lime juice
½ tsp. minced garlic
⅛ tsp. salt
⅛ tsp. pepper
4 brioche hamburger
  buns, split and toasted
4 lettuce leaves

1. In a large bowl, whisk yogurt and tandoori seasoning until blended. Add chicken and turn to coat. Cover and refrigerate at least 30 minutes or overnight, turning occasionally.

2. Meanwhile, in a small bowl, combine the slaw ingredients. Refrigerate, covered, until serving. For sauce, combine yogurt, mint, lime juice, garlic, salt and pepper. Refrigerate, covered, until serving.

3. Preheat air fryer to 375°. Drain chicken, discarding marinade. Place the chicken in a single layer on greased tray in air-fryer basket. Cook until a thermometer reads 170°, 8-10 minutes on each side. Spread sauce over toasted bun tops. On each bun bottom, layer lettuce, chicken and slaw. Replace tops.

1 sandwich: 384 cal., 15g fat (5g sat. fat), 114mg chol., 559mg sod., 32g carb. (9g sugars, 4g fiber), 28g pro. **Diabetic exchanges:** 3 lean meat, 2 starch, 2 fat.

CHAPTER 9

SWEETS & DESSERTS

If your air fryer isn't already your favorite kitchen gadget, get ready to be amazed. No need to turn on the oven when you have these quick and easy recipes for the best sweet treats at your fingertips.

APPLE CAKE WITH BUTTERMILK SAUCE

This apple cake is easier than you think. By baking it in an air fryer, you don't have to heat up the oven, which is a lifesaver when you're in the midst of holiday baking.
—Sarita Gelner, Waunakee, WI

PREP: 40 MIN. • COOK: 50 MIN. + COOLING • MAKES: 12 SERVINGS

1½ cups apple cider or juice

APPLE TOPPING
- 2 cups chopped peeled tart apples
- 3 Tbsp. sugar
- 1 Tbsp. orange juice
- ½ tsp. ground cinnamon
- ½ tsp. ground cloves

CAKE
- ½ cup butter, melted
- ¾ cup sugar
- 2 large eggs, room temperature
- 1½ tsp. vanilla extract
- 1¼ cups cake flour
- 1 tsp. baking powder
- ¼ tsp. salt
- ½ cup sour cream

BUTTERMILK SAUCE
- ¾ cup sugar
- 6 Tbsp. butter, cubed
- ⅓ cup buttermilk
- 2 tsp. light corn syrup
- ¼ tsp. baking soda
- ¼ tsp. vanilla extract

1. In a small saucepan, bring cider a boil; cook until the liquid is reduced to about ¼ cup, 15-20 minutes. Remove from the heat and cool.

2. Preheat air fryer to 325°. In a large bowl, combine the apples, sugar, orange juice, cinnamon and cloves; toss to coat. For cake batter, in a large bowl, beat the butter, sugar, eggs, vanilla and cooled cider reduction until well blended. In another bowl, whisk cake flour, baking powder and salt; add to the butter mixture alternately with sour cream, beating after each addition just until combined.

3. Transfer a greased 8-in. springform pan that fits in the air fryer. Spoon apple mixture over batter. Cook until a toothpick inserted in center comes out clean, 50-60 minutes; cover tightly with foil if top browns too quickly. Cool 15 minutes on a wire rack.

4. For sauce, in a small saucepan combine the sugar, butter, buttermilk, corn syrup and baking soda. Cook and stir over medium heat until bubbly, 4-6 minutes. Remove from the heat; stir in vanilla. Pour sauce over cake. Serve warm. Refrigerate any leftovers.

1 piece: 345 cal., 16g fat (10g sat. fat), 74mg chol., 255mg sod., 48g carb. (35g sugars, 1g fiber), 3g pro.

CREME BRULEE

There's something so elegant and regal about creme brulee, but it's basically just a baked custard. I love how easy it is to make in an air fryer.

—Joylyn Trickel, Helendale, CA

PREP: 15 MIN. • COOK: 25 MIN. + COOLING • MAKES: 4 SERVINGS

- 2 cups heavy whipping cream
- 5 large egg yolks
- 6 Tbsp. sugar
- ½ tsp. vanilla extract
- 2 Tbsp. brown sugar

AIR-FRYING TIP
When using a blow torch to caramelize the sugar, work slowly and keep the ramekins on a baking sheet to protect your countertops.

1. In a large saucepan, combine cream, egg yolks and sugar. Cook and stir over medium heat until mixture reaches 160° or is thick enough to coat the back of a metal spoon. Stir in vanilla.

2. Preheat air fryer to 275°. Transfer to four 8-oz. ramekins or custard cups. In batches if necessary, place ramekins in air fryer. Cook until centers are just set (mixture will jiggle), roughly 20-25 minutes. Cool for 10 minutes; cover and refrigerate for at least 4 hours.

3. One hour before serving, sprinkle each with 1½ tsp. brown sugar. Using a kitchen torch or blow torch, caramelize sugar until dark golden brown. Or broil 8 in. from the heat until sugar is caramelized, 4-7 minutes. Refrigerate leftovers.

1 creme brulee: 577 cal., 49g fat (30g sat. fat), 366mg chol., 45mg sod., 30g carb. (29g sugars, 0 fiber), 7g pro.

BEST EVER CHEESECAKE

This cheesecake is truly something special. For extra flair,
serve it with fresh whipped cream or your favorite fruit topping.
—*Howard Koch, Lima, OH*

PREP: 20 MIN. • COOK: 45 MIN. + CHILLING • MAKES: 8 SERVINGS

1¼ cups graham
      cracker crumbs
⅓ cup butter, melted
¼ cup sugar

FILLING/TOPPING
2 pkg. (8 oz. each) cream
   cheese, softened
2 large eggs, room
   temperature, lightly beaten
⅔ cup sugar, divided
2 tsp. vanilla extract, divided
   Dash salt
1 cup sour cream
   Whipped cream, optional

1. Preheat air fryer to 325°. In a bowl, combine graham cracker crumbs, butter and sugar. Pat into the bottom and 1 in. up the sides of an 8-in. springform pan that fits into the air fryer. Chill while preparing filling.

2. For filling, beat cream cheese and eggs in a bowl on medium speed for 1 minute. Add ⅓ cup sugar, 1 tsp. vanilla and salt. Continue beating until well blended, about 1 minute. Pour mixture into crust.

3. Cook until the center is almost set, 25-30 minutes. Cool for 10 minutes. For topping, combine sour cream and remaining sugar and vanilla in a small bowl; spread over cheesecake. Cook 15 minutes longer. Cool on wire rack 10 minutes. Loosen sides from pan with a knife. Cool 1 hour longer. Refrigerate 3 hours or overnight. If desired, serve with whipped cream.

1 piece: 504 cal., 36g fat (20g sat. fat), 145mg chol., 357mg sod., 40g carb. (30g sugars, 1g fiber), 7g pro.

WHY YOU'LL LOVE IT...
"I made this cheesecake for Thanksgiving and it was delicious! The only addition that I made was a half teaspoon of lemon juice. This cheesecake never cracks! Easy to make and it is truly 'Best Ever Cheesecake.'"
—FLEETWOOD2, TASTEOFHOME.COM

FRIED COOKIES

Deep-fried Oreos are quickly becoming a county fair favorite. Now you can make them at home quickly, easily and mess free.
—*Margarita Torres, Bayamon, Puerto Rico, AE*

PREP: 10 MIN. + FREEZING • COOK: 5 MIN./BATCH • MAKES: 1½ DOZEN

18 Oreo cookies
1 large egg, room
   temperature
¼ cup 2% milk
¼ tsp. almond extract
1 cup biscuit/baking mix
   Confectioners' sugar

1. On each of eighteen 4-in. wooden skewers, thread 1 cookie, inserting pointed end of skewer into filling if desired. Freeze until firm, about 1 hour.

2. Preheat air fryer to 350°. Cut pieces of parchment to fit the bottom of the air fryer. In a shallow bowl, whisk together egg, milk and extract; add biscuit mix and stir just until moistened. Dip cookie into the biscuit mixture to coat both sides; shake off excess. Place a sheet of parchment in air fryer; spray parchment with nonstick cooking spray. In batches, arrange cookies in a single layer ½-in. apart, placing 1 cookie in each corner of the paper so it doesn't fly around during cooking.

3. Cook until golden brown, 5-7 minutes. Dust with confectioners' sugar before serving.

1 cookie: 84 cal., 3g fat (1g sat. fat), 11mg chol., 115mg sod., 13g carb. (5g sugars, 0 fiber), 1g pro.

APPLE CRISPS

This dish tastes delicious with any apple but our favorite are the Honeycrisp apples we pick at our local orchard every September. We are always looking for new ways to use the apples and this has become a favorite.

—Sabrina Olson, Otsego, MN

PREP: 20 MIN. • COOK: 15 MIN. • MAKES: 6 SERVINGS

¼ cup butter
3 Tbsp. honey
½ tsp. apple pie spice
½ tsp. vanilla extract
1 cup crushed raw almonds
1 cup old-fashioned oats

FILLING

3 unpeeled medium apples, cut into ½-in. pieces
3 Tbsp. sugar
1 Tbsp. lemon juice
1 tsp. apple pie spice
   Vanilla ice cream, optional

1. Mix butter, honey, apple pie spice and vanilla. In a large bowl, combine almonds and oats; toss with butter mixture until well coated. Press 2 Tbsp. almond mixture onto bottoms of each of 6 greased 6-oz. ramekins.

2. Preheat air fryer to 325°. For filling, combine apples, sugar, lemon juice and pie spice. Spoon filling evenly into ramekins. Place ramekins in air fryer. Cook until apple mixture is bubbly, 8-10 minutes. Top with remaining oat mixture. Cook until topping is golden brown and the fruit is tender, about 5 minutes. Serve warm; if desired, top with ice cream.

1 crisp: 308 cal., 17g fat (6g sat. fat), 20mg chol., 62mg sod., 38g carb. (24g sugars, 5g fiber), 5g pro.

AIR-FRYING TIP

To test for doneness, insert a clean toothpick into the center of a cupcake. If it comes out clean, or with a few crumbs, the cupcakes are ready to come out of the air fryer. If the toothpick comes out with wet batter, the cupcakes need more time to bake.

MOCHA CUPCAKES

These luscious chocolate cupcakes smell wonderful while they're in the air fryer. If you have the drawer-type air fryer you'll need to use individual silicone cupcake liners. If you have a big enough air fryer, a 6-cup muffin tin should fit in nicely.
—*Mary Bilyeu, Ann Arbor, MI*

PREP: 25 MIN. • COOK: 15 MIN./BATCH + COOLING • MAKES: 1 DOZEN

1 cup sugar
½ cup cold brewed coffee
½ cup canola oil
2 large eggs, room temperature
3 tsp. cider vinegar
3 tsp. vanilla extract
1½ cups all-purpose flour
⅓ cup baking cocoa
1 tsp. baking soda
½ tsp. salt

MOCHA FROSTING
3 Tbsp. milk chocolate chips
3 Tbsp. semisweet chocolate chips
⅓ cup butter, softened
2 cups confectioners' sugar
1 to 2 Tbsp. brewed coffee
½ cup chocolate sprinkles

1. Preheat air fryer to 325°. In a large bowl, beat sugar, coffee, oil, eggs, vinegar and vanilla until well blended. In a small bowl, combine flour, cocoa, baking soda and salt; gradually beat into coffee mixture until blended.

2. For muffin tins that fit in air fryer, fill paper-lined muffin cups three-fourths full. Otherwise, use silicone muffin cups. Place muffin cups in a single layer in air fryer. Cook until a toothpick inserted in center comes out clean, roughly 11-13 minutes. Cool completely before removing from muffin cup.

3. For frosting, in a microwave, melt chocolate chips and butter; stir until smooth. Transfer to a large bowl. Gradually beat in the confectioners' sugar and enough coffee to reach the desired consistency. Pipe frosting onto cupcakes. Top with sprinkles; gently press to adhere.

1 cupcake: 414 cal., 19g fat (5g sat. fat), 45mg chol., 260mg sod., 59g carb. (43g sugars, 1g fiber), 4g pro.

PINEAPPLE UPSIDE-DOWN CHEESECAKE

Taking inspiration from my mom's pineapple upside-down cake, I added a cheesecake layer and baked it in an air fryer. It is so delicious and so easy.
—*Marilyn McGinnis, Citrus Heights, CA*

PREP: 20 MIN. • COOK: 25 MIN. + CHILLING • MAKES: 4 SERVINGS

¾ cup packed brown sugar
4 slices canned pineapple (one 8-oz. can)
4 maraschino cherries

FILLING
1 pkg. (8 oz.) cream cheese, softened
½ cup confectioners' sugar
2 tsp. all-purpose flour
1 tsp. vanilla extract
1 large egg, room temperature, lightly beaten
¼ cup crushed pineapple, well drained

CRUST
1 Tbsp. butter
⅓ cup graham cracker crumbs
¼ tsp. ground cinnamon

1. Preheat air fryer to 300°. Sprinkle brown sugar into a greased 8-in. cake pan that fits into air fryer. Arrange the pineapple in a single layer over brown sugar; place a cherry in the center of each pineapple slice.

2. For filling, in a large bowl, beat the cream cheese and confectioners' sugar until smooth. Beat in flour and vanilla. Add egg; beat on low speed just until blended. Fold in crushed pineapple. Spoon over fruit.

3. Cook until center is almost set, 20-25 minutes. Cool on a wire rack 10 minutes. Loosen sides from pan with a knife. Cool 1 hour longer. Refrigerate overnight, covering when completely cooled.

4. For crust, in a small skillet, melt butter over medium-low heat. Add cracker crumbs and cinnamon; cook and stir until toasted, 4-6 minutes. Cool. Just before serving, top cheesecake with toasted crumbs, pressing to adhere. Invert cheesecake onto a serving plate.

1 piece: 554 cal., 25g fat (14g sat. fat), 111mg chol., 269mg sod., 80g carb. (72g sugars, 1g fiber), 6g pro.

PEAR POT PIES

I love to make pot pies when pears are in season. I love them so much more than apples because I think they have a better flavor.
—*Bee Engelhart, Bloomfield Township, MI*

PREP: 20 MIN. • COOK: 20 MIN. • MAKES: 4 SERVINGS

2 Tbsp. butter, divided
2 Tbsp. sugar
1 Tbsp. cornflake crumbs
1 Tbsp. brown sugar
¼ tsp. ground ginger
2 cups finely chopped peeled Anjou pears
2 cups finely chopped peeled Bartlett pears
1 Tbsp. orange juice
½ sheet frozen puff pastry, thawed
   Vanilla ice cream

1. Grease bottoms and sides of four 8-oz. ramekins with 1 Tbsp. butter (do not butter rims).

2. In a small bowl, mix sugar, cornflake crumbs, brown sugar and ginger. In a large bowl, toss pears with orange juice. Add crumb mixture and toss to combine. Divide mixture among ramekins; dot with remaining 1 Tbsp. butter.

3. Preheat air fryer to 325°. Unfold pastry; cut into ½-in. strips. Arrange over ramekins in a lattice pattern, trimming to fit. Gently press ends onto ramekin rims.

4. Place ramekins in air fryer. Cook until filling is bubbly and pastry is golden brown, 20-25 minutes. Serve warm with ice cream.

1 pot pie: 343 cal., 15g fat (6g sat. fat), 62mg chol., 177mg sod., 50g carb. (24g sugars, 7g fiber), 5g pro.

TEST KITCHEN TIP: Thaw puff pastry at room temperature for about 20 minutes before handling. Handle as little as possible to avoid stretching and tearing.

HOMEMADE CHURROS

Serve these cinnamon-sugar treats fresh and hot with a cup of
coffee or hot chocolate. They're sure to become a family favorite!
—Taste of Home *Test Kitchen*

PREP: 15 MIN. + CHILLING • COOK: 15 MIN. • MAKES: 1 DOZEN

½ cup water
½ cup 2% milk
1 Tbsp. canola oil
¼ tsp. salt
1 cup all-purpose flour
1 large egg, room
   temperature
¼ tsp. grated lemon zest
½ cup sugar
¼ tsp. ground cinnamon
   Cooking spray

1. In a large saucepan, bring water, milk, oil and salt to a boil. Add flour all at once and stir until a smooth ball forms. Transfer to a large bowl; let stand for 5 minutes.

2. Beat on medium-high speed for 1 minute or until the dough softens. Add egg and lemon zest; beat for 1-2 minutes. Set aside to cool. Insert a large star tip in a pastry bag; fill bag with dough. Pipe the dough into 4-in. strips 1-in. apart onto parchment. Chill for 1 hour.

3. Preheat air fryer to 375°. Transfer piped churros to air fryer; spritz with cooking spray. Cook until golden brown, roughly 15-20 minutes. Combine sugar and cinnamon; sprinkle over churros. Serve warm.

1 churro: 97 cal., 2g fat (0 sat. fat), 17mg chol., 60mg sod., 17g carb. (9g sugars, 0 fiber), 2g pro.

AIR-FRYING TIP
You can make the dough for these churros a day or two in advance—just keep it refrigerated in an airtight container. Because churros are best served warm, though, we recommend air-frying them right before serving.

ORANGE CRANBERRY CAKE

This cake has an Old World flavor and texture. It's a little coarser than most American cakes but that's what gives it its rustic charm.
—*Ninette Holbrook, Orlando, FL*

PREP: 25 MIN. • COOK: 15 MIN. + COOLING • MAKES: 8 SERVINGS

⅓ cup sugar
⅓ cup canola oil
2 large eggs, room temperature
1 Tbsp. grated orange zest
1 Tbsp. orange juice
⅓ cup all-purpose flour
⅓ cup cream of wheat or farina flour
½ tsp. salt
¼ tsp. baking powder
⅓ cup dried cranberries, chopped
¼ cup sliced almonds

ORANGE GLAZE
¾ cup confectioners' sugar
1 Tbsp. orange juice
2 tsp. 2% milk
 Grated orange zest, optional

1. Preheat air fryer to 325°. Grease an 8-in. round baking pan that will fit in air fryer.

2. In a large bowl, beat sugar, oil, eggs, orange zest and juice until well blended. In another bowl, whisk flour, cream of wheat, salt and baking powder; gradually beat into the oil mixture. Stir in the dried cranberries.

3. Transfer to prepared pan; sprinkle with almonds. Cook until a toothpick inserted in center comes out clean, 15-20 minutes.

4. Combine glaze ingredients; pour over warm cake. Cool for 10 minutes before serving. If desired, sprinkle with orange zest.

1 piece: 263 cal., 12g fat (1g sat. fat), 47mg chol., 182mg sod., 36g carb (25g sugars, 1g fiber), 4g pro.

PEANUT BUTTER COOKIES

An iconic American cookie, this version is so easy to mix up and bakes even faster in the air fryer. Cookie cravings can be satisfied in mere minutes now.
—*Maggie Schimmel, Wauwatosa, WI*

PREP: 15 MIN. • COOK: 5 MIN./BATCH • MAKES: 3 DOZEN

1 large egg, room temperature, beaten
1 cup sugar
1 cup creamy peanut butter

1. In a large bowl, mix all ingredients. Roll level tablespoonfuls of dough into balls. Flatten with a fork.

2. Preheat air fryer to 400°. In batches, place balls 1 in. apart in greased air fryer. Cook until lightly browned, 3-4 minutes. Allow to cool slightly on the pan and remove to wire racks to cool.

1 cookie: 66 cal., 4g fat (1g sat. fat), 5mg chol., 32mg sod., 7g carb. (6g sugars, 0 fiber), 2g pro.

TEST KITCHEN TIP: You'll know your peanut butter cookies are done when they appear soft in the center—a little underbaked, but not raw—with golden edges. The cookies will firm up as they cool.

A

Apple Cake with Buttermilk
    Sauce 232
Apple Crisps 240
Asian Turkey Burger
    with Apple Slaw 221
Asparagus-Stuffed
    Chicken Rolls 159

B

Bacon-Wrapped
    Asparagus 22
Bacon-Wrapped Filets 192
Bacon-Wrapped Scallops
    with Pineapple Quinoa . . . 111
Bacon-Wrapped Tater Tots . . . 30
Baked Potatoes 81
Balsamic Zucchini 98
Banana Bread 53
Barbecue Chicken 167
Barbecue Chicken Legs . . . 163
Beef Jerky 200
Beef Turnovers 187
Best Ever Cheesecake 236
Black Bean
    Chimichangas 107
Bone-In Pork Chops with
    Rhubarb 136
Bratwurst Sandwiches
    with Beer Gravy 210
Breakfast Potatoes 49
Brown Sugar Ham 144
Brussels Sprouts
    with Bacon 93

Buffalo Cauliflower 98
Buffalo Chicken Wings 37
Butternut Squash Tacos . . . 124

C

Cabbage & Onions 74
Cheesy Quesadillas 213
Chicken Cutlet 168
Chicken Fajitas 175
Chicken Parmesan 152
Chicken Piccata Pockets . . . 148
Chicken Yakitori 151
Chicken-Fried Steaks 199
Cinnamon Doughnuts 54
Cinnamon Tea Rolls 42
Copycat Fried Chicken
    Sandwich 209
Cornflake Chicken 176
Cornish Hens 171
Cowboy Casserole 188
Crab au Gratin
    Spread 13
Crab Rangoon 26
Creme Brulee 235
Crispy Calamari 38
Crispy Chicken Wings 17
Crispy Orange Chicken 160

E

Easy Salisbury Steak 195
Eggs Lorraine 65

F

Fish Tacos 119
Fried Cookies 239

G

Garlic Bread 73
Garlic Corn on the Cob 86
Garlicky Potato Latkes 90
General Tso's Chicken Sandwich
    with Broccoli Slaw 214
Ginger Butternut Squash . . . 73
Grilled Cheese
    Sandwiches 222

H

Ham & Brie Pastries 18
Ham & Leek Pies 135
Ham Steak with
    Pineapple Salsa 128
Hard-Boiled Eggs 50
Hearty Meat Loaf 184
Hoisin Chicken Wraps 218
Homemade Breakfast
    Bites 61
Homemade Churros 248
Homemade Falafel 120
Honey Sweet Potatoes 94
Honey-Coconut Sticky
    Buns 62

K

Kale Chips 34

L

Lasagna for 2 115
Lemon Pepper Broccoli 78
Loaded Hash Browns 58

M

Masala Chicken
  Sandwiches 229
Mediterranean Turkey
  Potpies 172
Mocha Cupcakes 243
Mom's Olive Burgers 217
Mozzarella Sticks 21

O

Onion Crescent Rolls 89
Orange Cranberry Cake . . . 251

P

Parmesan Potato
  Wedges 97
Peanut Butter Cookies 252
Pear Pot Pies 247
Pecan Chicken Sliders 225
Pineapple Upside-Down
  Cheesecake 244
Pizza Puffs 33
Pork Loin Roast 139
Pork Tenderloin 131
Pumpkin Shakarpara 29

R

Raspberry Crumble Coffee
  Cake 45
Roast Beef with Horseradish
  Sauce 183
Rotisserie Chicken 156

S

Salmon Patties 108
Sausage Bacon Bites 46
Sausage Pizzas 140
Savory Sausage Patties 57
Scotch Eggs 10
Seasoned Plantains 82
Spicy Turkey Tenderloin . . . 164
Stuffed Peppers 191
Stuffed Pork Burgers 206
Stuffed Sweet Potatoes 70
Stuffed Zucchini 180
Sweet Potato Chips . . . . , 14

T

Taco Kabobs 196
Taco Puffs 203
Tahitian Breakfast Treats . . . 66
Tailgate Sausages 226
Tempeh Bacon 116
Thai Pork Satay 132
Thin Pork Chops 143
Thyme-Roasted Carrots 85
Tilapia Fillets 123
Turkey Wings 155
Twice-Baked Potato 101

V

Vegan Butter Cauliflower . . . 104
Vegetarian Stuffed
  Mushrooms 25
Veggie Burgers 112

Z

Zucchini Fries 77

COMMON AIR-FRYER MISTAKES

They promise extra-crispy food without all the extra fat, but if you don't use your air fryer properly, results may be less than dazzling.

Too much stuff on the counter.
It might be small—and mighty—but air fryers need their space. That's because these mini ovens rely on a constant flow of air to move the high-temp heat around the food for all-over crispness. Make sure your air fryer has at least 5 inches of space on all sides. And keep it on a stable surface, so the vibration won't send it tumbling onto the floor.

Not preheating the air fryer.
Like an oven, an air fryer needs to be hot to properly cook the moment the door shuts. If it's too cold, the final food may suffer. Check your recipe's suggested temperature before getting started. Go ahead and turn the air fryer on, so it is plenty hot when you're ready to use it. It won't take long—that small space can reach the right temperature in under five minutes.

Using too much oil.
Most air fryers call for only a teaspoon or two of oil. If too much is added, you won't get the results you're looking for. Remember that an air fryer is not a deep fryer. But it achieves similar results by circulating very hot air around food as it bakes.

Not using any oil.
You can have too much oil—and you can have too little. Most recipes will recommend the amount that's right for that dish, but when in doubt, give your food a quick spritz. Oil is a great medium to transfer heat. Spritzing a little bit of nonstick oil spray will help the food get crisp and brown.

The foods are too wet.

Deep fryers can expel moisture from foods like batters, but an air fryer isn't capable of that. Don't put limp, wet veggies in an air fryer, as they will not crisp up properly. Instead, use your air fryer to quickly crisp already breaded or crunchy foods, such as breaded chicken tenders or Brussels sprouts.

The foods are too light.
An air fryer's moving air means lighter foods could float and fly around inside the appliance. You don't want something lightweight like spinach, as it starts to fry, to get caught in the heating coil and start to burn.

Too much food in the basket.

The machine needs air around it, and the food does, too. If you overcrowd the basket, the food won't have enough exposed surface area. Where the hot air meets the surface of the food and any oil is where the cooking (and flavor) happens. Because air fryers cook quickly, you can cook in small batches—and that will ensure each piece has the best possible flavor and texture.

The food is too small.
Food that is too small could slip right through the slots in the air-fryer basket and fall onto a heating element. The pieces will burn quickly, which could fill your food—and your kitchen—with fumes and smoke. Keep all of your ingredients about the size of a Brussels sprout. When in doubt, drop the food in the basket and give it a shake over the sink. If anything slips out, don't put it in the air fryer.

Fatty foods drip.
You might have purchased an air fryer to complement a lower-fat eating plan, but you can also use it to fry up high-fat favorites like burgers, sausages and bacon. Before you hit the start button, make sure you put water in the bottom of the cavity under the frying basket. This way, when fat drips onto the hot surface, it will hit water—not hot metal—preventing fat from burning and creating a smoky mess.

Cooking in the air fryer without cleaning it.
A dirty air fryer can be dangerous for your stomach and your nose. There's a much higher risk of food contamination if you do not clean your air fryer between uses.